PREGNANCY DEVOTIONAL FOR EXPECTANT MOTHERS

5-MINUTE DEVOTIONS TO BOND WITH YOUR UNBORN BABY, UPLIFT YOU THROUGH ANXIOUS MOMENTS, & HANDLE THE UPS & DOWNS OF EACH TRIMESTER WITH FAITH

BIBLICAL TEACHINGS

FAB PUBLISHING

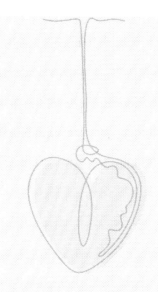

_____

TO

_____

FROM

Copyright © 2024 by Biblical Teachings -All rights reserved.

No part of this book may be reproduced in any form or by any electronic or mechanical means, including information storage and retrieval systems, without written permission from the author, except for the use of brief quotations in a book review.

Under no circumstances will any blame or legal responsibility be held against the publisher, or author, for any damages, reparation, or monetary loss due to the information contained within this book, either directly or indirectly.

Legal Notice:

This book is copyright protected. It is only for personal use. You cannot amend, distribute, sell, use, quote, or paraphrase any part, or the content within this book, without the author or publisher's permission.

Disclaimer Notice:

Please note that the information contained within this document is for educational and entertainment purposes only. All effort has been executed to present accurate, up-to-date, reliable, complete information. No warranties of any kind are declared or implied. Readers acknowledge that the author is not rendering legal, financial, medical, or professional advice. The content within this book has been derived from various sources. Please consult a licensed professional before attempting any techniques outlined in this book.

By reading this document, the reader agrees that under no circumstances is the author responsible for any losses, direct or indirect, that are incurred due to the use of the information in this document, including, but not limited to, errors, omissions, or inaccuracies.

CONTENTS

The Journey of Motherhood — ix

1. Coping with Morning Sickness & Extreme Fatigue — 1
2. The Emotional Rollercoaster — 3
3. Loneliness Despite the Joy — 5
4. Overwhelmed by the Reality of Pregnancy — 7
5. Celebrating Small Milestones — 9
6. Love Your Changing Body — 14
7. Support from Loved Ones — 16
8. Managing Food Aversions & Intense Cravings — 18
9. First Ultrasound Excitement — 20
10. God's Perfect Plan — 22
11. Keeping Your Pregnancy a Secret Early On — 26
12. Understanding Baby's Development — 28
13. Nurturing Your Relationship with Your Partner — 30
14. Handling Unsolicited Advice — 32
15. Experiencing God's Presence — 34
16. Praying for Your Baby's Future — 38
17. Maintaining Hope Through Challenges — 40
18. Daily Gratitude — 42
19. Connecting with Other Expectant Mothers — 44
20. Adjusting to a Growing Belly — 50
21. Feeling Baby's First Movements — 52
22. Back Pain & Discomfort — 54
23. Completing Your Daily To-Dos Despite Pregnancy Fatigue — 56
24. Confronting Labor Anxiety — 60
   Light the Path for Another Expectant Mother — 62
25. Keeping the Spark Alive — 64
26. Loving Your Pregnancy Body — 66
27. Preparing for Maternity Leave — 68
28. Dealing with Pregnancy Brain — 70
29. Handling Unwanted Comments About Your Body — 74
30. Enjoying the Second Trimester Glow — 76

31. Creating the Perfect Nursery	78
32. Experiencing Emotional Stability	81
33. Handling Unexpected Medical Concerns	86
34. Stress-Free Baby Registry	88
35. Mom-to-Mom	90
36. Making the Most of Parental Classes	92
37. Counting Down the Days	96
38. God's Strength for Labor	98
39. Creating a Spiritual Environment	100
40. Emotional Prep for the Big Day	102
41. Welcoming Your Baby	106
42. Finding Peace Amidst Pre-Birth Chaos	108
43. Pregnancy Insomnia	110
44. Last-Minute Baby Prep	112
45. Third Trimester Discomforts	116
46. Cherishing the Last Days	118
47. Facing Fears of the Unknown	120
48. Faith Over Finances	122
Pass On the Blessings	124
And So, The Journey Continues...	127

BIBLE STUDY
-Starter Kit-

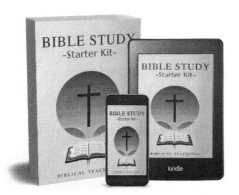 

Discover a **<u>Simple</u>**, **<u>Powerful</u>** Way to Study **<u>The Bible</u>**

- *No More Guesswork* - Learn to Explore the Bible **with Confidence** and Clarity.

- Discover a Study Method That *Fits Seamlessly into Your Busy Life* - **Without the Overwhelm**.

- **Build a Bible Study Routine** *You'll Actually Look Forward To* - Not Just Another Task on Your To-Do List.

<u>SCAN THE QR CODE</u> FOR YOUR <u>FREE</u> COPY

THE JOURNEY OF MOTHERHOOD

Welcome to '*The Pregnancy Devotional for Expectant Moms.*' Pregnancy is a remarkable journey, one that transforms not just your body, but your heart and soul as well. Whether you are in your first trimester or nearing the birth of your baby, this devotional is designed to accompany you through each stage with spiritual comfort and practical insights.

Within these pages, you will find 48 devotions, thoughtfully crafted to support you through the unique experiences and emotions of pregnancy. These devotions are grounded in scripture, and tailored to the real needs and challenges expectant mothers face.

Pregnancy not only brings about significant change, but also a mix of excitement, uncertainty, and profound joy. This devotional aims to offer you a sanctuary of peace and reflection during this special time. Each devotion is an invitation to deepen your relationship with God, reflect on your journey, and prepare your heart and home for the arrival of your baby.

How to Use This Book:

1. **Go at Your Own Pace:** Pregnancy is a unique journey for every woman. Set aside time each day or week to read a devotion, as your schedule and energy levels allow. Follow the order or choose the one that speaks to you most at any given time. Feel free to date each entry to keep track of your journey. Don't worry if you miss a day or week—God's guidance is always available, and this book is here to support you whenever you need it.
2. **Begin with Scripture:** Start by reading the title and the relevant Bible verse to set the context for your reflection.
3. **Engage with the Devotional Insight:** Dive into the devotional insight and let yourself connect with the experiences and wisdom shared. These insights are designed to resonate with your own journey of motherhood.
4. **Reflect and Relate:** After the devotion, take a moment to reflect on the lessons learned and how they apply to your life as an expectant mother. This section bridges the insight with your personal experiences and feelings. Remember to follow the reflection prompts for the full benefit.
5. **Prayer Time:** End your session with the provided prayer, opening your heart to God and seeking His guidance and strength for your pregnancy journey.

Throughout these devotions, you will explore themes of faith, hope, love, and preparation. From coping with morning sickness and dealing with unsolicited advice to feeling your baby's first movements and preparing for labor, these devotions are designed to support and uplift you.

This is a sacred time for you and your growing family. May these devotions become a source of comfort, inspiration, and growth as you prepare to welcome your baby into the world. Remember, God's love for you is unwavering, and His plans for you and your baby are filled with hope and a future.

Take the first step today. Open your heart, embrace the journey, and let's walk this path together. This beautiful new chapter is ready to unfold...

Welcome to the journey of motherhood.

P.S. *All scripture quotations are taken from the Holy Bible, New International Version (NIV), unless otherwise noted.*

FIRST TRIMESTER
What To Expect

SCAN ME

Physical Changes:

Morning sickness, fatigue, breast changes, frequent urination, food cravings, spotting and cramping, constipation.

Emotional Changes:

Mood swings, anxiety, excitement.

Baby's Development:

Weeks 1-4: Fertilization and implantation.
Weeks 5-8: Heartbeat and major organ formation.
Weeks 9-12: Limb and facial feature development.

Health & Nutrition Tips

Prenatal Vitamins: Essential for you and your baby.

Balanced Diet: Include fruits, vegetables, lean proteins, whole grains.

Hydration: Try to drink 8-12 cups (64-96 ounces) of water each day for optimal health for both you and your baby.

Important Milestones

Positive Pregnancy Test

First Ultrasound (6-12 weeks)

Sharing the News

FIRST TRIMESTER MILESTONES

Document Your Journey

Positive Pregnancy Test

Date: _____

Feelings: _____

Photo:

First Ultrasound (6-12 weeks)

Date: _____

Baby's Heartbeat: _____

Feelings: _____

Photo:

Sharing the News

Date: _____

How did you share? _____

Reactions: _____

1

COPING WITH MORNING SICKNESS & EXTREME FATIGUE

"I sought the Lord, and he answered me; he delivered me from all my fears."

— PSALM 34:4

Do you find yourself gripped by the fear of miscarriage? The anxiety can be overwhelming, casting a shadow over the joy of expecting a new life. This fear is natural, and you are not alone. Hannah, a faithful woman in the Bible, knew this fear all too well. She deeply longed for a child and prayed earnestly for one. Her heart was heavy with the possibility of never becoming a mother.

In her distress, Hannah sought the Lord. She poured out her heart, expressing her fears and anxieties. God heard her prayers and blessed her with a son, Samuel. Hannah's story teaches us the importance of turning to God in our moments of deepest fear. Her faith and persistence in prayer were key to overcoming her anxieties.

When fear grips your heart, remember Hannah's example. Seek the Lord with your worries and let His peace comfort you. It's okay to feel afraid, but don't let that fear control you. Lean into your faith, surround yourself with supportive friends and family, and remember that God is with you every step of the way. Sometimes, simply acknowledging your fears and speaking them aloud in prayer can provide immense relief.

Practical steps can also help manage these fears. Consider speaking with a healthcare provider about your concerns, joining a support group for expectant mothers, or engaging in calming activities like prenatal yoga or meditation. Each of these can provide a tangible sense of peace and community.

God is aware of your desires and fears. Trust in His plan, even when the future feels uncertain. His grace is sufficient, and He will deliver you from your fears, just as He did for Hannah. Embrace the journey with faith and hope, knowing that you are cradled in His loving arms.

Mom's Moments

Share your fears and anxieties about the possibility of miscarriage in a prayer journal. Ask God for peace and trust in His plan for you and your baby.

Short Prayer

Dear God, Help me release my fears about miscarriage. Grant me peace and trust in Your perfect plan for my baby and me. Amen.

_____

_____

_____

_____

2

THE EMOTIONAL ROLLERCOASTER

"Do not be anxious about anything, but in every situation, by prayer and petition, with thanksgiving, present your requests to God. And the peace of God, which transcends all understanding, will guard your hearts and your minds in Christ Jesus."

— PHILIPPIANS 4:6-7

Are you experiencing a rollercoaster of emotions during your pregnancy? It's common to feel joy one moment and anxiety the next. These emotional highs and lows can be overwhelming, but they are a normal part of this transformative journey.

During my pregnancies, I often found myself swinging between ecstatic excitement and deep worry. One moment, I was overjoyed imagining the future with my little one; the next, I was gripped by fears of the unknown. This ebb and flow of emotions is something many expectant mothers experience, and it's perfectly natural.

Philippians 4:6-7 reminds us to bring all our anxieties to God through prayer and thanksgiving. When you feel joyful, celebrate and give thanks to God for the blessing of your baby. When you feel anxious or low, present your worries to Him, trusting that His peace will guard your heart and mind. God's peace transcends all understanding and is available to you in every situation.

Managing these emotions involves acknowledging them and seeking God's presence. Take time each day to reflect on your feelings and invite God into those moments. Whether through prayer, reading scripture, or simply sitting in His presence, allow His peace to wash over you. Some practical steps include keeping a gratitude journal, practicing deep breathing exercises, or engaging in a hobby that brings you joy.

Also, don't hesitate to reach out for support. Talk to your partner, friends, or a counselor about what you're feeling. Sometimes, just expressing your emotions aloud can provide clarity and relief. Remember, emotional highs and lows are part of the beautiful complexity of bringing new life into the world.

Remember, you are not alone in this journey. God is with you, ready to offer comfort and peace. Embrace each emotion as it comes, knowing that God's peace is available to you at all times.

Mom's Moments

Describe the range of emotions you've experienced this week. Write about how you can turn to God in both joyful and challenging moments.

Short Prayer

Dear God, thank You for being with me through every emotion. Help me to seek Your peace in both joyful and challenging times. Amen.

3

LONELINESS DESPITE THE JOY

"Be strong and courageous. Do not be afraid or terrified because of them, for the Lord your God goes with you; he will never leave you nor forsake you."

— DEUTERONOMY 31:6

Have you ever felt a wave of loneliness wash over you, even amidst the joy of discovering you're expecting? I remember the early weeks of my pregnancy when, despite the excitement, I felt incredibly alone. It seemed like no one could truly understand what I was going through.

There were moments when I sat quietly, pondering the new life growing inside me, yet felt an overwhelming sense of isolation. Friends and family were supportive, but I still felt like I was carrying the weight of this new responsibility by myself. It was during these times that I clung to the promise in Deuteronomy 31:6. God's assurance that He would never leave me nor forsake me became my anchor.

Reflecting on this verse, I realized that I was never truly alone. God was with me in every early ultrasound, every flutter, and every sleepless night. His presence provided a sense of companionship that no human could offer. I began to invite Him into my daily routines, speaking to Him as I navigated the early symptoms and uncertainties.

If you're feeling lonely despite the joy, remember that God is right there with you. Lean into His presence and let His companionship fill the gaps. Share your heart with Him, and allow His love to comfort and uplift you.

Mom's Moments

Connect with a close friend or family member who has experienced pregnancy. Share your feelings of loneliness and ask for their advice and support. Write about how their understanding and empathy helped ease your loneliness and brought you joy.

Short Prayer

Dear God, thank You for always being with me. Please comfort me in times of loneliness and fill my heart with Your presence. Amen.

_____

_____

_____

_____

_____

_____

_____

4

OVERWHELMED BY THE REALITY OF PREGNANCY

"Come to me, all you who are weary and burdened, and I will give you rest. Take my yoke upon you and learn from me, for I am gentle and humble in heart, and you will find rest for your souls. For my yoke is easy and my burden is light."

— MATTHEW 11:28-30

Do you ever feel overwhelmed by the sheer magnitude of being pregnant? The initial changes, responsibilities, and anticipation can sometimes feel like too much to handle. In these early weeks, the reality of what is happening can truly sink in, and it's normal to feel utterly overwhelmed.

There are days when the endless to-do lists, the first prenatal appointments, and the physical changes can seem insurmountable. You might worry about being a good mother, about the health of your baby, and about all the unknowns that lie ahead. It is during these moments of overwhelm that Jesus' invitation in Matthew 11:28-30 becomes a lifeline. He calls to you, offering rest and peace in His gentle and humble heart.

Imagine laying your burdens at His feet, one by one. You don't have to carry the weight of pregnancy alone. Jesus offers to share your load, to give you rest for your soul. Take comfort in His gentleness and humility, and allow yourself to take things one day at a time, trusting in His strength.

If you're feeling overwhelmed, know that it's okay to take a step back and breathe. Allow yourself to rest in God's presence. He invites you to come to Him, to find rest and peace. Lean on Him, and let His gentle heart guide you through this early season.

Mom's Moments

Identify and describe the specific responsibilities or changes to come that feel most overwhelming. Reflect on how these challenges make you feel and how you can manage them. Write a prayer asking for rest and peace in God's presence, seeking strength and calm in these moments.

Short Prayer

Dear God, thank You for offering me rest. Please help me to lay my burdens at Your feet and find peace in Your presence. Amen.

_____

_____

_____

_____

5

CELEBRATING SMALL MILESTONES

"The Lord your God is with you, the Mighty Warrior who saves. He will take great delight in you; in his love he will no longer rebuke you, but will rejoice over you with singing."

— ZEPHANIAH 3:17

Have you taken a moment to celebrate the small milestones in your pregnancy? It's easy to get caught up in the bigger picture and forget to find joy in the little moments. Each milestone, no matter how small, is a precious gift and a reminder of God's hand in your journey.

In the first trimester, these milestones might include seeing your baby for the first time during an ultrasound or hearing the heartbeat for the first time. Even the confirmation of your pregnancy test is a small, joyous milestone worth celebrating. These moments may seem small, but they are profound indicators of the miracle growing inside you. God rejoices over you and your baby, delighting in these milestones just as you do.

Take time to acknowledge and celebrate each of these moments. Whether it's the relief of a good doctor's appointment, the first sign of a baby bump, or the joy of sharing your pregnancy news with loved ones, these are all opportunities to see God's love and handiwork in your life. Allow these small joys to uplift your spirit and deepen your gratitude.

In these small milestones, you can find a reflection of God's delight in you. He is with you in every step, rejoicing over you and your baby. Embrace these moments, knowing that they are part of a beautiful journey that God is guiding you through.

Mom's Moments

List your recent milestones, no matter how small. Reflect on the joy they bring and how they are signs of God's active involvement in your pregnancy journey.

Short Prayer

Dear God, thank You for the small milestones that bring joy. Help me to see Your hand in each moment and celebrate Your presence in my journey. Amen.

_____

_____

_____

_____

_____

EATING GUIDE + LIFESTYLE ADJUSTMENTS

Healthy Eating Guide and Simple Recipes

Fueling Your Pregnancy

Tips for Maintaining a Balanced Diet:
- **Eat Small, Frequent Meals:** Helps manage nausea and keeps energy levels steady.
- **Include a Variety of Foods:** Fruits, vegetables, whole grains, lean proteins, and dairy.
- **Stay Hydrated:** Drink at least 8-10 glasses of water daily.
- **Prenatal Vitamins:** Ensure you're getting essential nutrients like folic acid, iron, and calcium.
- **Limit Caffeine and Avoid Alcohol:** Opt for water, herbal teas, and decaf beverages.

Morning Sickness Relief:
- **Ginger Tea**: Helps soothe nausea.
- **Crackers or Dry Toast**: Eat first thing in the morning.
- **Peppermint Tea**: Can alleviate nausea symptoms.
- **Bananas**: Easy on the stomach and rich in potassium.

Simple Recipes for Morning Sickness Relief

Ginger and Lemon Tea:

Ingredients:
1. 4 inches of fresh ginger, sliced, or grated
2. 1 lemon sliced (how much you use depends on personal preference)
3. 1 pot of water
4. Honey to taste

Instructions:
1. Boil water in a pot. Once its boiling turn off the heat.
2. Add sliced / grated ginger and lemon slices then cover and steep for 30 mins.
3. Strain and add honey if desired.
4. Drink warm.

Banana and Almond Smoothie:

Ingredients:
1. 1/4 cup almonds
2. 1 banana, sliced
3. 1/2 cup milk (almond, or other)
4. 5-6 ice cubes
5. 1 teaspoon honey

Instructions:
1. Blend almonds into a buttery texture.
2. Add the remaining ingredients and blend.
3. Serve immediately.

FOOD CRAVINGS AND AVERSIONS TRACKER

Cravings:

Date	Food Craved	Intensity of Craving	How Satisfied You Feel After Eating
_____	_____	Mild / Moderate / Strong	_____
_____	_____	Mild / Moderate / Strong	_____
_____	_____	Mild / Moderate / Strong	_____
_____	_____	Mild / Moderate / Strong	_____
_____	_____	Mild / Moderate / Strong	_____

Aversions:

Date	Food Avoided	Intensity of Aversion	Alternative Foods Tried
_____	_____	Mild / Moderate / Strong	_____
_____	_____	Mild / Moderate / Strong	_____
_____	_____	Mild / Moderate / Strong	_____
_____	_____	Mild / Moderate / Strong	_____
_____	_____	Mild / Moderate / Strong	_____

6

LOVE YOUR CHANGING BODY

"Do you not know that your bodies are temples of the Holy Spirit, who is in you, whom you have received from God? You are not your own; you were bought at a price. Therefore honor God with your bodies."

— 1 CORINTHIANS 6:19-20

Do you find yourself struggling with the physical changes that come with pregnancy? Your body is undergoing incredible transformations, and it's normal to feel a mix of emotions about these changes. Even Mary, the mother of Jesus, faced this reality as she adjusted to her pregnancy.

Think of Mary, a young woman chosen by God to carry the Savior of the world, experiencing her body changing in ways she never anticipated. She might have felt self-conscious about her growing belly or the discomforts of pregnancy. Yet, Mary embraced these changes, knowing that her body was fulfilling a divine purpose.

Your body is also fulfilling a divine purpose. The changes you're experiencing are a testament to the life growing within you. Stretch marks, weight gain, and swelling can be daunting, but they are signs of your body's remarkable ability to nurture and sustain life. While it can be challenging to embrace these changes, remember that your body is a temple of the Holy Spirit, and you are honoring God with each transformation.

Take time to appreciate your body's strength and resilience. Celebrate its ability to adapt and support your baby. Instead of focusing on the discomfort or appearance, focus on the miracle that your body is creating. Engage in self-care practices that honor your body, such as gentle exercise, nourishing foods, and restful sleep.

Embrace your body with gratitude and honor its purpose. You are part of a beautiful, divine process that reflects God's love and creativity.

Mom's Moments

Detail the physical changes you've noticed in your body recently, then express your thoughts about them. Pray for acceptance and appreciation of your body's strength and purpose.

Short Prayer

Dear God, thank You for the strength and resilience of my body. Help me to accept and appreciate the changes as part of Your divine plan. Amen.

_____

_____

_____

7

SUPPORT FROM LOVED ONES

"Two are better than one, because they have a good return for their labor: If either of them falls down, one can help the other up. But pity anyone who falls and has no one to help them up."

— ECCLESIASTES 4:9-10

Do you feel the strength that comes from the support of your loved ones? Pregnancy can be a time of great joy but also a period of vulnerability and need for support. The early stages, in particular, can be challenging with the physical and emotional adjustments you are experiencing. This is when the presence of a loving support system becomes invaluable.

Think about the people in your life who are walking this journey with you—your partner, family, friends, and even your healthcare providers. Their encouragement, assistance, and presence can make a significant difference. Ecclesiastes 4:9-10 beautifully illustrates the power of support and companionship. When you feel weak or overwhelmed, your loved ones can help lift you up, providing the strength you need to keep going.

Having someone to lean on, to share your fears and joys, brings comfort and reassurance. Their prayers, words of encouragement, and practical help are tangible expressions of God's love and care for you. Whether it's a friend bringing over a meal, a family member helping with chores, or your partner holding your hand during a doctor's visit, these acts of support are blessings to be cherished.

Take a moment to appreciate these people and the role they play in your life. Reflect on how their support strengthens you, and make sure to express your gratitude. Knowing you have a support system can lighten the load and make the journey more joyful.

Mom's Moments

Write about the support you receive - who it's from, what they do, and how it strengthens you. Pray for appreciation and gratitude towards your support system.

Short Prayer

Dear God, thank You for the loved ones who support me. Help me to appreciate their care and express my gratitude for their presence in my life. Amen.

_____

_____

_____

_____

8

MANAGING FOOD AVERSIONS & INTENSE CRAVINGS

"So whether you eat or drink or whatever you do, do it all for the glory of God."

— 1 CORINTHIANS 10:31

Are you struggling with food aversions and cravings? The first trimester often brings unexpected changes in your appetite and food preferences, which can be both amusing and challenging. I remember when I was pregnant, certain foods I once loved suddenly made me nauseous, while I developed an intense craving for foods I rarely ate.

These experiences can be puzzling and sometimes frustrating. I found myself avoiding the smell of coffee, which I had always enjoyed, and craving citrus fruits like they were going out of style. Navigating these changes required a lot of patience and creativity in meal planning.

Reflecting on 1 Corinthians 10:31, I realized that even in these small daily choices, I could honor God. By focusing on maintaining a balanced diet and listening to my body's needs, I learned to make healthier choices that supported both my health and my baby's development. This verse encouraged me to be mindful of how I approached eating, seeking to glorify God through my choices and attitude.

To help manage aversions and cravings, keep a variety of healthy snacks on hand that appeal to you, such as fresh fruits, nuts, or whole grain crackers. Drinking plenty of water and eating small, frequent meals can also help keep nausea at bay. Experiment with different foods to find what works for you and remember to be kind to yourself during this time.

If you're experiencing similar food aversions and cravings, try to embrace the changes with a sense of humor and grace. Listen to your body and find nutritious alternatives that satisfy your cravings without compromising your health. Remember that God is with you in these small, daily decisions, guiding you towards what's best for you and your baby.

Mom's Moments

Reflect on and journal your experiences with food aversions and cravings. Describe what a normal day of eating has been like for you recently - what foods you crave, and what ones you can't stand. Write a prayer for health and balance in your diet.

Short Prayer

Dear God, thank You for guiding me through these changes in my appetite. Help me to make healthy choices and find balance in my diet for my baby's sake. Amen.

9

FIRST ULTRASOUND EXCITEMENT

"For you created my inmost being; you knit me together in my mother's womb. I praise you because I am fearfully and wonderfully made; your works are wonderful, I know that full well."

— PSALM 139:13-14

Are you feeling the excitement and anticipation of your first ultrasound? It's a moment filled with wonder and joy as you see the tiny life growing inside you for the first time. This profound experience brings to mind the biblical story of Elizabeth, who felt her baby, John the Baptist, leap in her womb in recognition of Mary and Jesus. This story beautifully captures the miraculous and intimate connection between a mother and her unborn child.

Elizabeth's baby leaping in her womb was a sign of joy and recognition of God's miraculous work. Similarly, your first ultrasound is a profound reminder of God's handiwork. Seeing your baby's heartbeat and movements on the screen is a tangible testament to the life being wonderfully and fearfully knit together by God.

This incredible moment can bring tears of joy and an overwhelming sense of gratitude. It's a reminder of the preciousness of life and the intricate care God has taken in creating your baby. Take a moment to soak in this experience and thank God for this miracle.

During my own pregnancies, the first ultrasound was always a deeply moving experience. The sight of that tiny heartbeat was a powerful reminder of God's creative power and His intimate involvement in the process of life. It filled me with awe and reinforced my trust in His plans for my family.

As you prepare for this special moment, remember that it's a celebration of the life growing within you. Embrace the joy and let it strengthen your bond with your baby and deepen your faith in God's loving care.

Mom's Moments

Reflect on the emotions you experienced leading up to and during your first ultrasound. Write a heartfelt prayer of gratitude for the miracle you witnessed and the reassurance it provided.

Short Prayer

Dear God, thank You for the joy and wonder of seeing my baby for the first time. I am grateful for this miraculous moment and Your handiwork. Amen.

_____

_____

_____

_____

10

GOD'S PERFECT PLAN

"For I know the plans I have for you," declares the Lord, "plans to prosper you and not to harm you, plans to give you hope and a future."

— JEREMIAH 29:11

Do you ever find yourself worrying about the future and what it holds for you and your baby? It's natural to have concerns and uncertainties, but finding peace in God's plan can bring immense comfort. Jeremiah 29:11 reminds us that God has a plan for us—one that is filled with hope and a future.

Trusting in God's plan means letting go of our fears and anxieties and placing our confidence in His perfect will. This can be challenging, especially when faced with the unknowns of pregnancy and motherhood. However, embracing this trust can bring a profound sense of peace.

Think about the times when God has guided you through difficult situations in the past. His faithfulness and love have always been there, leading you to where you are now. Reflecting on these moments can strengthen your trust in His plan for your pregnancy and your baby's future.

Encourage yourself to lean into God's promises. When doubts arise, remind yourself of Jeremiah 29:11. God's plans are to prosper you and not to harm you, to give you hope and a future. Trust that He is guiding every step of your journey, and His peace will guard your heart and mind.

Mom's Moments

Write down your current worries and uncertainties. Next, list ways you've experienced God's faithfulness. Compare the two lists and pray for peace in God's plan for you and your baby.

Short Prayer

Dear God, thank You for Your perfect plan for me and my baby. Help me to trust in Your guidance and find peace in Your promises. Amen.

_____

_____

_____

_____

_____

_____

_____

_____

LIFESTYLE ADJUSTMENTS FOR A HEALTHY PREGNANCY

Rest and Relaxation

Rest & Relaxation:

1. **Sleep:**

   - **Aim for 7-9 Hours:** Prioritize getting a full night's sleep to support your body and baby.
   - **Comfortable Sleep Environment:** Use pillows to support your body and maintain a comfortable temperature.

2. **Naps:**

   - **Short Naps:** 15-30 minute naps during the day can help combat fatigue.
   - **Rest Periods:** Take regular breaks to rest and recharge, especially during busy days.

Avoid Harmful Substances:

1. **Caffeine:**

   - **Limit Intake:** Keep caffeine consumption to 200 mg per day (about one 12 oz cup of coffee).
   - **Healthy Alternatives:** Opt for decaffeinated tea, herbal tea, or water.

2. **Alcohol and Smoking:**

   - **Avoid Completely:** Refrain from consuming alcohol and smoking during pregnancy to protect your baby's health.

Doctor Visits:

1. **Regular Check-Ups:**

   - **Prenatal Appointments:** Keep up with your scheduled prenatal appointments to monitor your health and your baby's development.
   - **Discuss Concerns:** Always discuss any concerns or symptoms with your healthcare provider.

Stress Management

Stress Management Techniques:

1. **Mindfulness and Meditation:**
   - **Daily Practice:** Set aside 10-15 minutes each day for mindfulness or meditation to manage stress and anxiety.
   - **Guided Sessions:** Use apps or online videos for guided meditation sessions tailored for expectant mothers.

2. **Deep Breathing Exercises:**
   - **Calming Technique:** Practice deep breathing exercises to calm the mind and reduce tension.
   Example Exercise: Inhale deeply through your nose, hold for a few seconds, and exhale slowly through your mouth.

3. **Support System:**
   - **Lean on Loved Ones:** Seek emotional support from friends, family, and support groups.
   - **Join a Community:** Consider joining a prenatal support group or online community to share experiences and advice.

Triggers & Coping Strategies

Date	Stress Trigger	Coping Strategy

11

KEEPING YOUR PREGNANCY A SECRET EARLY ON

"There is a time for everything, and a season for every activity under the heavens."

— ECCLESIASTES 3:1

Have you found it difficult to keep your pregnancy a secret in the early weeks? I remember the excitement and joy bubbling inside me when I first discovered I was pregnant, but I also felt the weight of keeping this precious news to myself. Those early weeks can be a mixture of joy and caution, as you wait for the right time to share your news with loved ones.

Reflecting on Ecclesiastes 3:1, I realized that there is indeed a time for everything. This scripture reminded me to trust in God's timing and to be patient. Keeping the pregnancy a secret can be challenging, especially when you're bursting with excitement. But it can also be a special time to bond with your baby and to pray over your pregnancy before the world knows.

Many people choose to wait until the end of the first trimester to share their news, as the risk of miscarriage decreases significantly after this period. Others might wait until after their first midwife appointment or ultrasound, when they have seen the baby and heard the heartbeat. Ultimately, the perfect moment is when you feel comfortable and confident.

During my pregnancies, I found comfort in talking to God about my excitement and fears. I prayed for patience and wisdom in knowing when to share the news. I also cherished the intimate moments I had with my baby, knowing that this was a unique season just for the two of us.

If you're struggling with keeping your pregnancy a secret, lean on God for strength and guidance. Trust that there will be a perfect time to share your joy with others. Meanwhile, enjoy this special, private time and let it strengthen your connection with your baby and with God.

Mom's Moments

Reflect on the reasons you want to keep your pregnancy a secret in the early weeks. Write about the challenges and benefits of waiting to share the news. Pray for patience, wisdom, and the right timing to share your joy.

Short Prayer

Dear God, thank You for this precious gift. Grant me patience and wisdom as I wait to share my news. Help me to cherish this special time. Amen.

12

UNDERSTANDING BABY'S DEVELOPMENT

"My frame was not hidden from you when I was made in the secret place, when I was woven together in the depths of the earth."

— PSALM 139:15-16

Isn't it hard not to be in awe of the miraculous development of your baby? Each stage of your baby's growth is a testament to God's incredible design and care. The Bible tells us that God is intricately involved in the creation of life, knitting us together in the womb with loving precision.

Consider the profound imagery in Psalm 139:15-16. It beautifully describes how God is aware of every detail of our being, even when we are hidden from the world. Your baby's development is not random; it is a carefully orchestrated process by the Creator Himself. From the formation of tiny fingers and toes to the beating of a tiny heart, each detail is a reflection of God's artistry.

Elizabeth, the mother of John the Baptist, experienced a moment of profound recognition of God's handiwork when her baby leapt in her womb at the sound of Mary's greeting. This leap was not just a physical reaction but a joyful acknowledgment of the presence of Jesus. Similarly, each kick and movement you feel is a reminder of the life being woven together inside you. Take time to marvel at this miracle and to thank God for His incredible creation.

Understanding your baby's development can deepen your appreciation for the miracle of life. It can also enhance your sense of connection with your baby. As you learn about each stage of growth, allow it to fill you with awe and gratitude for God's wondrous work.

Mom's Moments

Create a weekly journal to document your baby's development. Each week, write down new milestones, physical changes, and any movements you feel. Reflect on the miracle of life growing inside you and write a prayer of gratitude for your baby's progress.

Short Prayer

Dear God, thank You for the miracle of my baby's development. I am in awe of Your creation and grateful for this blessing. Amen.

_____

_____

_____

_____

_____

_____

13

NURTURING YOUR RELATIONSHIP WITH YOUR PARTNER

"Husbands, love your wives, just as Christ loved the church and gave himself up for her."

— EPHESIANS 5:25

Are you noticing how your relationship with your partner is evolving during this pregnancy? As you both prepare for parenthood, it's important to nurture and strengthen your bond. This time of transition can bring you closer together as you support each other through the changes and challenges.

Ephesians 5:25 reminds us of the deep, sacrificial love that Christ has for the church, which serves as a model for the love between partners. This kind of love involves patience, understanding, and mutual respect. As you journey through pregnancy, take time to invest in your relationship.

Communicate openly about your hopes, fears, and expectations. Share the joys and concerns of this new chapter. Practical steps like setting aside regular time for each other, even if it's just a quiet evening at home, can make a big difference. Attend prenatal appointments together, make decisions about your baby's future as a team, and pray together, asking God to guide and strengthen your relationship.

During my pregnancy, my partner and I found that dedicating time to discuss our feelings and to pray together brought us closer. We supported each other through the ups and downs, and this unity prepared us for the journey ahead.

Remember, your relationship is the foundation for your growing family. By nurturing it, you're creating a strong, loving environment for your baby.

Mom's Moments

Plan a special date night with your partner each week. After each date, write about how you felt, what you enjoyed, and any meaningful conversations you had. Reflect on the ways you can continue to nurture and strengthen your relationship during this time.

Short Prayer

Dear God, thank You for my partner. Help us to grow stronger and more united as we prepare for parenthood together. Amen.

_____

_____

_____

_____

_____

_____

14

HANDLING UNSOLICITED ADVICE

"Listen to advice and accept discipline, and at the end you will be counted among the wise."

— PROVERBS 19:20

Have you ever felt overwhelmed by the unsolicited advice you receive during pregnancy? Friends, family, and even strangers often feel compelled to share their opinions, which can sometimes be more overwhelming than helpful. I remember receiving a flood of advice, much of it conflicting, when I was expecting my first child.

There was one instance where I was bombarded with opinions about what I should and shouldn't eat. While I knew everyone meant well, it left me feeling confused and stressed. I realized that I needed to handle these interactions with grace and discernment. Proverbs 19:20 reminds us of the value of listening to advice, but it also implies the need for discernment in what we accept.

I started by politely thanking people for their advice, recognizing their good intentions. Then, I would evaluate the information, considering whether it aligned with my values, my doctor's recommendations, and what felt right for me and my baby. This approach helped me to filter out unnecessary stress and focus on what truly mattered.

Handling unsolicited advice with grace doesn't mean you have to follow every piece of it. It's about acknowledging the advice, discerning its value, and responding with kindness. Remember, God has equipped you with the wisdom and instincts to make the best decisions for you and your baby.

Mom's Moments

Recall a specific piece of unsolicited advice you received and note how it made you feel. Reflect on your reaction and how you handled it. Pray for the discernment to manage such interactions with grace and wisdom.

Short Prayer

Dear God, thank You for the wisdom to discern helpful advice. Help me to handle unsolicited advice with grace and make the best decisions for my baby. Amen.

_____

_____

_____

_____

_____

_____

15

EXPERIENCING GOD'S PRESENCE

"You make known to me the path of life; you will fill me with joy in your presence, with eternal pleasures at your right hand."

— PSALM 16:11

Are you taking the time to seek and feel God's presence during your pregnancy? This season of life, filled with anticipation and change, offers a unique opportunity to draw closer to God. His presence can bring comfort, joy, and a deep sense of peace as you navigate the journey of motherhood.

Reflect on Psalm 16:11, which speaks of the joy and eternal pleasures found in God's presence. Even amidst the physical and emotional challenges of pregnancy, God is with you, guiding and supporting you. Take a moment to recall specific instances where you have felt His closeness—perhaps during a quiet moment of prayer, a comforting word from a friend, or the awe-inspiring experience of hearing your baby's heartbeat for the first time.

Seeking God's presence can be as simple as setting aside time each day to pray, meditate on His Word, or just sit quietly and invite Him into your thoughts and feelings. As you do, you'll find that His presence fills you with joy and strength, helping you to face each day with confidence and peace.

During my own pregnancies, I found that intentionally seeking God's presence transformed my experience. It helped me to feel more connected to my baby and more at peace with the changes happening in my body and life.

Mom's Moments

Each day, write down one way you have felt God's presence during your pregnancy on a small piece of paper and place it in a jar. At the end of your pregnancy, read through all your blessings and reflect on how God has been with you throughout the journey.

Short Prayer

Dear God, thank You for Your constant presence. I am grateful for the moments when I feel Your closeness and the joy You bring into my life. Amen.

_____

_____

_____

_____

_____

_____

EXERCISE AND SELF-CARE TIPS

Safe Exercises for the First Trimester

Safe Exercises:

1. **Walking:**
   - **Daily Walks**: Aim for 20-30 minutes of walking daily. It's a great low-impact exercise that helps maintain fitness.
   - **Stay Hydrated**: Drink plenty of water before, during, and after your walk.

2. **Prenatal Yoga:**
   - **Gentle Stretching**: Helps improve flexibility and reduce pregnancy-related discomfort.
   - **Focus on Breathing**: Incorporate deep breathing exercises to enhance relaxation.

3. **Swimming:**
   - **Low-Impact**: Swimming provides a full-body workout without putting stress on your joints.
   - **Stay Cool**: It's a refreshing way to stay active and cool, especially in warmer weather.

Self-Care Routines:

1. **Relaxation Techniques:**
   - **Warm Baths**: Take a warm (not hot) bath with Epsom salts to soothe sore muscles.
   - **Aromatherapy**: Use essential oils like lavender to create a calming atmosphere.

2. **Pampering Yourself:**
   - **Skincare**: Keep your skin hydrated with moisturizing lotions and oils.
   - **Hair and Nails**: Treat yourself to a gentle manicure or a relaxing hair treatment.

3. **Mental Wellness:**
   - **Reading**: Spend time reading books that you enjoy.
   - **Hobbies**: Engage in hobbies that bring you joy and relaxation.

Personal Wellness Goals

Setting Personal Wellness Goals:

1. **Physical Health:**
   - **Goal**: Walk for 20 minutes daily
   - **Action Plan**: Schedule walks in the morning or evening, track progress in a journal.

2. **Mental Health:**
   - **Goal**: Practice prenatal yoga twice a week.
   - **Action Plan**: Join a prenatal yoga class or follow online sessions, keep a yoga log.

3. **Emotional Well-Being:**
   - **Goal**: Spend 15 minutes each day in meditation or mindfulness.
   - **Action Plan**: Set a daily reminder, use a meditation app, and journal your experiences.

Wellness Goals Tracker

Date	Wellness Goal	Action Plan	Progress

16

PRAYING FOR YOUR BABY'S FUTURE

"For I know the plans I have for you," declares the Lord, "plans to prosper you and not to harm you, plans to give you hope and a future."

— JEREMIAH 29:11

Have you taken time to pray and think about your hopes for your baby's future? The anticipation of a new life brings many dreams and wishes for your child. Reflecting on these hopes and lifting them up to God can be a powerful way to connect with Him and to trust in His promises.

Consider the story of Hannah in the Bible. She fervently prayed for a child and, when God answered her prayer, she dedicated her son Samuel to the Lord's service. Hannah's prayers for Samuel didn't stop after his birth; she continued to pray for his future, trusting God's plan for his life. Her faith and dedication serve as a beautiful example of how we can pray for our children's futures.

As you reflect on Jeremiah 29:11, remember that God has a plan for your baby—one filled with hope and a future. Take time to pray for your child, asking God to guide their steps, protect them, and help them to grow into the person He has created them to be. Trust in His promises and His love for your child.

During my pregnancies, praying for my baby's future was a special way to connect with God and to surrender my worries and dreams to Him. It brought me peace, knowing that God was already holding my child's future in His hands.

Mom's Moments

Spend some quiet time visualizing your hopes and dreams for your baby's future. Write down three things you hope your child will experience or achieve, and why these hopes are important to you

Short Prayer

Dear God, thank You for the plans You have for my baby. Please guide and protect my child, and help them to grow in Your love. Amen.

_____

_____

_____

_____

_____

_____

_____

17

MAINTAINING HOPE THROUGH CHALLENGES

"May the God of hope fill you with all joy and peace as you trust in him, so that you may overflow with hope by the power of the Holy Spirit."

— ROMANS 15:13

How do you maintain hope through the challenges of pregnancy? There were times during my pregnancies when I felt overwhelmed by fears and uncertainties. Whether it was worrying about the health of my baby or dealing with physical discomforts, maintaining hope was sometimes a struggle.

Romans 15:13 became a beacon of light for me. This verse reminded me that God is the source of all hope, and it's through His power that we can find joy and peace, even in difficult times. I learned to lean on God's promises and to trust that He was with me, guiding me through each challenge.

One particular challenge was dealing with morning sickness. It was relentless and made even simple tasks seem impossible. But each day, I prayed for strength and hope, asking God to help me see beyond the discomfort to the joy of the life growing inside me. Gradually, I began to feel a sense of peace and hope that carried me through.

In addition to prayer, there are other methods that can help maintain hope. Surround yourself with a supportive community—friends, family, and other expectant mothers who can offer encouragement and share their experiences. Engage in activities that bring you joy and relaxation, such as reading, walking, or listening to uplifting music. Reflecting on positive affirmations and keeping a journal of your thoughts and feelings can also be powerful tools to stay hopeful.

If you are facing challenges in your pregnancy, remember that God is your source of hope. Trust in Him, and allow His joy and peace to fill your heart. Know that He is with you and your baby, providing strength and comfort every step of the way.

Mom's Moments

Develop a personal mantra or phrase that encapsulates hope for you. Repeat this mantra during difficult moments. Reflect on how this practice helps you stay hopeful and focused on positive outcomes.

Short Prayer

Dear God, thank You for being my source of hope. Help me to trust in You and to find joy and peace in Your presence. Please bless my baby and surround us with Your love and protection. Amen.

_____

_____

_____

_____

18

DAILY GRATITUDE

"Give thanks in all circumstances; for this is God's will for you in Christ Jesus."

— 1 THESSALONIANS 5:18

Do you make it a habit to practice gratitude each day? The journey of pregnancy can be filled with both joy and challenges, and finding moments of gratitude can help you see God's goodness in every circumstance. Gratitude shifts our focus from what we lack to the abundant blessings God has provided.

Reflecting on 1 Thessalonians 5:18, we are reminded to give thanks in all circumstances. This doesn't mean that every moment will be easy or joyful, but it encourages us to look for God's hand in every situation. Even on the hardest days, there is something to be grateful for—a supportive partner, a kind word from a friend, the beauty of a sunset, or the miracle of feeling your baby move.

Practicing gratitude daily can transform your perspective and fill your heart with joy. Start or end each day by writing down a few things you are grateful for. It could be as simple as a delicious meal, a moment of rest, or a reassuring doctor's visit. Over time, you'll begin to see God's goodness more clearly and feel His presence more deeply.

During my pregnancies, keeping a gratitude journal helped me stay positive and focused on the blessings around me. It reminded me of God's faithfulness and filled me with peace, even during challenging times.

Mom's Moments

Keep a daily gratitude log. At the end of each day, write down 3 things you are grateful for that day. Reflect on how this practice helps you notice God's goodness in the everyday moments.

Short Prayer

Dear God, thank You for the many blessings You provide each day. Help me to cultivate a heart of gratitude and to see Your goodness in every moment. Please nurture my baby with Your love and grace. Amen.

_____

_____

_____

_____

_____

_____

_____

19

CONNECTING WITH OTHER EXPECTANT MOTHERS

"And let us consider how we may spur one another on toward love and good deeds, not giving up meeting together, as some are in the habit of doing, but encouraging one another—and all the more as you see the Day approaching."

— HEBREWS 10:24-25

Are you connecting with other expectant mothers during your pregnancy? Building relationships with women who are going through the same journey can provide invaluable support, encouragement, and understanding. The shared experiences and mutual encouragement can make the challenges of pregnancy more manageable and the joys even sweeter.

Hebrews 10:24-25 encourages us to spur one another on toward love and good deeds and to not give up meeting together. This verse highlights the importance of community and mutual support, especially during significant life events like pregnancy. By connecting with other expectant mothers, you create a network of support that can provide comfort, advice, and companionship.

Think about the moments when you've shared a laugh, a concern, or a piece of advice with another expectant mother. These interactions can be incredibly uplifting. Whether it's attending prenatal classes, joining a local or online support group, or simply having regular coffee dates with a friend who is also expecting, these connections can be a lifeline.

During my pregnancies, I found that talking to other expectant mothers helped me feel less isolated. We shared our worries and joys, exchanged tips, and supported each other through the ups and downs. These relationships enriched my pregnancy experience and provided me with lasting friendships.

If you haven't already, seek out opportunities to connect with other expectant mothers. These relationships can become a source of strength and encouragement, helping you to navigate this journey with a sense of community and shared understanding.

Mom's Moments

Join an online forum or social media group for expectant mothers. Participate in discussions, ask questions, and offer support. Reflect on how being part of a larger community helps you feel more connected and less isolated during your pregnancy.

Short Prayer

Dear God, thank You for the support of other expectant mothers. Help these relationships to grow and become a source of encouragement and strength

BIBLICAL TEACHINGS

for each of us. Please watch over our babies and bless our shared journey. Amen.

SECOND TRIMESTER
What To Expect

Physical Changes:

Growing belly, increased energy, reduced morning sickness, skin changes (potential for pregnancy glow or acne), back pain due to increased weight and shifting centre of gravity.

Emotional Changes:

Increased excitement, feeling more connected to your baby, mood swings, improved mood.

Baby's Development:

Weeks 13-16: Baby's muscles and bones are continuing to grow.

Weeks 17-20: Baby's movements may be felt; development of fingerprints.

Weeks 21-24: Rapid brain development and hearing improves; baby may respond to sounds

Important Milestones

First Kick

Anatomy Scan

Gender Reveal

SECOND TRIMESTER MILESTONES
Document Your Journey

First Kick:

Date: _____

Feelings: _____

Where did it happen? _____

Anatomy Scan:

Date: _____

Baby's Heartbeat: _____ bpm

Key Findings: _____
_____

Feelings: _____
_____

Photo:

Gender Reveal (if applicable):

Date: _____

How Did You Reveal? _____

Reactions: _____

Baby Bump Progress:

Date: _____

Description: _____
_____
_____
_____

Photo:

20

ADJUSTING TO A GROWING BELLY

"For you created my inmost being; you knit me together in my mother's womb. I praise you because I am fearfully and wonderfully made; your works are wonderful, I know that full well."

— PSALM 139:13-14

Have you noticed how your body is changing and growing as you progress through your pregnancy? The second trimester often brings significant physical changes, especially as your belly begins to expand more noticeably. I remember the excitement and, at times, the discomfort of adjusting to my growing belly.

Seeing my body change so dramatically was a mix of awe and challenge. There were days when I marveled at the incredible process of creating life, and other days when I struggled to feel comfortable in my own skin. Reflecting on Psalm 139:13-14 helped me find peace and appreciation for these changes. Knowing that God was knitting my baby together within me, I saw each change as part of His wonderful work.

As my belly grew, I experienced the reality of pregnancy more deeply. It became a visible sign of the miracle happening inside me. I found comfort in knowing that my body was doing exactly what it was designed to do. Embracing these changes, even when they were challenging, became easier when I focused on the purpose behind them.

If you're adjusting to a growing belly, take time to reflect on these changes and how they reflect God's handiwork. Celebrate your body's ability to nurture and grow new life. Embrace the changes with gratitude and awe for the incredible work God is doing within you.

Mom's Moments

Describe the most significant change you've noticed in your body recently. Write about your feelings toward this change and how it reflects the miracle of life growing within you.

Short Prayer

Dear God, thank You for the miracle of my growing belly. Help me to see Your handiwork in these changes and to embrace them with gratitude. Watch over my baby and bless their development. Amen.

_____

_____

_____

_____

_____

_____

_____

21

FEELING BABY'S FIRST MOVEMENTS

"Children are a heritage from the Lord, offspring a reward from him."

— PSALM 127:3

Isn't it an incredible moment when you first feel your baby move? The second trimester often brings this new and exciting experience. The Bible shares many stories of mothers who experienced the wonder of life within them. One such story is that of Sarah, Abraham's wife, who felt the miraculous blessing of her son Isaac growing inside her despite her old age.

Sarah's joy and amazement at her pregnancy, despite being well beyond childbearing years, remind us of the wonder and miraculous nature of new life. Feeling your baby move for the first time is a significant and joyous milestone. Each flutter, kick, and movement is a beautiful reminder of the life growing inside you.

When you first feel these movements, it can be a mix of surprise, joy, and wonder. I remember the first time I felt my baby move; it was like a gentle flutter, a delicate reminder of the tiny person growing within me. Each subsequent movement filled me with a sense of connection and anticipation for the future.

Take a moment to cherish this experience. Feeling your baby move is not only a sign of life but also a testament to God's wonderful creation. Allow this experience to deepen your bond with your baby and to fill your heart with gratitude for this precious gift.

Mom's Moments

Capture the exact moment you felt your baby move for the first time. Describe your emotions and the physical sensations. Write a few sentences expressing your gratitude for this incredible milestone.

Short Prayer

Dear God, thank You for the incredible experience of feeling my baby move. I am grateful for this new connection and the reminder of the life growing inside me. Bless my baby and ensure their healthy development. Amen.

_____

_____

_____

_____

_____

_____

_____

_____

22

BACK PAIN & DISCOMFORT

"He gives strength to the weary and increases the power of the weak."

— ISAIAH 40:29

Are you struggling with back pain and discomfort as your pregnancy progresses? This is a common experience, especially in the second trimester when your baby's growth puts extra pressure on your spine and muscles. It can be challenging to cope with these physical changes, but remember that God is your source of strength and comfort.

Isaiah 40:29 reminds us that God gives strength to the weary and increases the power of the weak. When you feel overwhelmed by pain and discomfort, turn to Him for relief and support. Simple practices such as gentle prenatal yoga, regular stretching, and using a supportive pillow while sleeping can help alleviate some of the discomfort.

Maintaining good posture and wearing comfortable, supportive shoes can also make a significant difference. Don't hesitate to ask your healthcare provider for recommendations on managing pain and discomfort during your pregnancy.

Remember, it's okay to take breaks and rest when needed. Your body is working hard to nurture and grow your baby, and it's essential to be kind to yourself during this time. Embrace the changes, knowing that God is with you, providing strength and relief.

Mom's Moments

Reflect on the times you've experienced back pain or discomfort during your pregnancy. Write down the methods you've tried to alleviate the pain and how effective they've been. You could even try some new ones. Pray for strength and comfort to manage these physical challenges.

Short Prayer

Dear God, thank You for Your strength and comfort. Please grant me relief from back pain and discomfort and help me to manage these changes with grace. Keep my baby safe and healthy. Amen.

_____

_____

_____

_____

_____

_____

23

COMPLETING YOUR DAILY TO-DOS DESPITE PREGNANCY FATIGUE

"Come to me, all you who are weary and burdened, and I will give you rest."

— MATTHEW 11:28

How are you managing the ups and downs of your energy levels during this pregnancy? The second trimester often brings a mix of vibrant days filled with energy and those where fatigue seems to take over. Balancing these fluctuations can be challenging, but it's important to listen to your body and give yourself the grace to rest.

Reflecting on Matthew 11:28, we are reminded that Jesus offers us rest and rejuvenation when we are weary. This verse has been a source of comfort for many, including myself. During my second trimester, I experienced days where I felt like I could take on the world, followed by days where I could barely keep my eyes open. It was a rollercoaster of energy levels, and finding a balance was key.

To manage these swings, I found it helpful to create a flexible routine that allowed for both activity and rest. Incorporating short naps, light exercises like walking, and healthy snacks throughout the day made a significant difference. Drinking plenty of water and practicing relaxation techniques, such as deep breathing or meditation, also helped maintain a sense of balance.

Remember, it's essential to prioritize rest and to be gentle with yourself. Pregnancy is a demanding journey, and your body is working hard to nurture and grow your baby. Embrace the moments of rest as opportunities to connect with God and to recharge your spirit. When you feel weary, take comfort in knowing that God invites you to find rest in Him.

Mom's Moments

Reflect on your current routine and how it accommodates your energy levels. Write about any adjustments you can make to ensure you are getting the rest you need. Consider creating a daily plan that includes times for activity and times for rest.

Short Prayer

Dear God, thank You for the promise of rest. Help me to balance my energy levels and to rest when needed. Please bless my baby with health and strength. Amen.

_____

_____

_____

_____

_____

_____

BABY REGISTRY ESSENTIALS

Baby Registry Checklist:

1. **Feeding:**
   - Bottles and Nipples
   - Breast Pump and Accessories
   - Formula (if needed)
   - Burp Cloths
   - High Chair

2. **Diapering:**
   - Diapers (Newborn and Size 1)
   - Wipes
   - Diaper Rash Cream
   - Changing Table or Pad
   - Diaper Bag

3. **Clothing:**
   - Onesies
   - Sleepers
   - Socks and Booties
   - Hats and Mittens
   - Swaddles

4. **Sleeping:**
   - Crib and Mattress
   - Crib Sheets
   - Sleep Sacks
   - Baby Monitor
   - White Noise Machine

5. **Bathing:**
   - Baby Bathtub
   - Towels and Washcloths
   - Baby Shampoo and Body Wash
   - Baby Lotion
   - Bath Toys

6. **Travel:**
   - Car Seat
   - Stroller
   - Baby Carrier or Sling
   - Diaper Bag
   - Travel Crib

7. **Health and Safety:**
   - Baby Thermometer
   - First Aid Kit
   - Baby Proofing Items (outlet covers, cabinet locks)
   - Nail Clippers
   - Pacifiers

NURSERY PLANNING

Tips for Nursery Planning:

- **Sketch Your Nursery:** Measure the room and start designing your nursery. Pinterest, and other online media are great for inspiration.
- **Theme and Colors:** Choose a theme that reflects your style and preferences. Opt for soothing colors to create a calming environment.
- **Furniture Placement:** Ensure the crib is away from windows and cords. Arrange furniture for easy access to essentials.
- **Storage Solutions:** Use shelves, baskets, and drawers to keep baby items organized and accessible.
- **Lighting:** Install dimmable lights for a soft, calming glow during nighttime feedings.
- **Personal Touches:** Add personalized items like name plaques, family photos, and handmade decorations.
- Create a space that is both functional and comforting.
- Include items that will grow with your baby.
- Don't forget to baby-proof the room for safety.

Key Purchases:

- **Furniture:**
  - ☐ Crib
  - ☐ Changing Table
  - ☐ Rocking Chair
  - ☐ Dresser

- **Decor:**
  - ☐ Wall Art
  - ☐ Rugs
  - ☐ Curtains
  - ☐ Mobiles (hanging decorations)

- **Storage:**
  - ☐ Baskets/Bins
  - ☐ Shelves
  - ☐ Closet Organizers

Shopping List:

1. _____
2. _____
3. _____
4. _____
5. _____
6. _____
7. _____
8. _____
9. _____
10. _____

24

CONFRONTING LABOR ANXIETY

> *"Do not be anxious about anything, but in every situation, by prayer and petition, with thanksgiving, present your requests to God. And the peace of God, which transcends all understanding, will guard your hearts and your minds in Christ Jesus."*
>
> — PHILIPPIANS 4:6-7

Are you feeling anxious about labor and delivery? It's normal to have fears and concerns about this significant event. Philippians 4:6-7 encourages us to bring our anxieties to God in prayer, trusting Him to provide peace and guidance.

Labor and delivery can be daunting, but remember that God is with you every step of the way. Reflect on the times when you have felt God's peace in other challenging situations. Trust that He will provide the same peace and strength during your labor.

Practical steps such as attending childbirth classes, creating a birth plan, and talking to your healthcare provider can help alleviate some of your anxiety. Remember to pray and ask God for peace and confidence as you approach your due date.

Mom's Moments

Identify your biggest anxieties about labor and delivery. Write about how you plan to cope with these fears. Reflect briefly on trusting the process and seeking peace during this significant moment.

Short Prayer

Dear God, please calm my anxieties about labor. Grant me peace and trust in Your plan for a safe and smooth delivery. Amen.

_____

_____

_____

_____

_____

_____

_____

_____

_____

_____

_____

LIGHT THE PATH FOR ANOTHER EXPECTANT MOTHER

"Give, and it will be given to you. A good measure, pressed down, shaken together and running over, will be poured into your lap."

— LUKE 6:38

Pregnancy is a remarkable journey, and I hope this book has been a source of strength, joy, and peace for you. As you continue to explore these devotions, I have a special request.

Would you help someone you've never met, even if you never got credit for it?

Who is this person you ask? They are like you. Or, at least, like you used to be. Less experienced, wanting to make a difference, and needing help, but not sure where to look.

Our mission is to make the journey of pregnancy a spiritually enriching experience for every expectant mother. Everything we do stems from that mission. And, the only way for us to accomplish that mission is by reaching...well...everyone.

This is where you come in. Most people do, in fact, judge a book by its cover (and its reviews). So here's my ask on behalf of a struggling expectant mother you've never met:

Please help that expectant mother by leaving this book a review.

Your gift costs no money and less than 60 seconds to make real, but can change a fellow expectant mother's life forever. Your review could help... ...one more mother find peace during sleepless nights. ...one more woman feel confident about her changing body. ...one more reader experience joy in the little moments. ...one more person build a spiritually nurturing environment for her baby. ...one more journey to a healthy and fulfilling pregnancy.

To get that 'feel good' feeling and help this person for real, all you have to do is **scan the QR code below:**

[Insert QR code]

[https://www.amazon.com/review/review-your-purchases/?asin=BOOKASIN]

If you feel good about helping a faceless expectant mother, you are my kind of person. Welcome to the club. You're one of us. Thank you from the bottom of my heart.

Your biggest fan,

Biblical Teachings

25

KEEPING THE SPARK ALIVE

"However, each one of you also must love his wife as he loves himself, and the wife must respect her husband."

— EPHESIANS 5:33

Are you finding ways to maintain intimacy with your partner during pregnancy? As your body changes and your focus shifts to preparing for your baby, it can be challenging to keep the connection with your partner strong. I remember how my partner and I navigated these changes, making intentional efforts to stay close.

Maintaining intimacy isn't just about physical closeness; it's about emotional and spiritual connection. We found that spending time together, sharing our thoughts and fears, and simply being present for each other helped us maintain our bond. Regular date nights, even if they were just quiet evenings at home, made a big difference.

Simple gestures like holding hands, giving each other massages, and expressing appreciation for one another strengthened our connection. Open communication is key—talk about your feelings and needs, and listen to your partner's as well. Maintaining intimacy is about finding ways to show love and respect, even amid the changes and challenges of pregnancy.

Reflect on the small ways you and your partner can nurture intimacy. Whether it's setting aside time for a walk together, cooking a meal, or just talking about your day, these moments help maintain a strong connection. Your relationship is the foundation of your growing family, so investing in it now will benefit all of you.

Mom's Moments

Reflect on the ways you and your partner have adapted to the changes brought by pregnancy. Write about one specific way you can support each other better. Consider creating a list of activities you both enjoy and commit to spending quality time together each week.

Short Prayer

Dear God, help us to maintain our closeness and understanding. Strengthen our bond as we prepare for the arrival of our baby. Amen.

26

LOVING YOUR PREGNANCY BODY

"Your beauty should not come from outward adornment, such as elaborate hairstyles and the wearing of gold jewelry or fine clothes. Rather, it should be that of your inner self, the unfading beauty of a gentle and quiet spirit, which is of great worth in God's sight."

— 1 PETER 3:3-4

How do you feel about the stretch marks and skin changes that come with pregnancy? These changes can be surprising and sometimes challenging to accept. However, they are also a testament to the incredible work your body is doing to bring new life into the world.

Reflecting on 1 Peter 3:3-4, we are reminded that true beauty comes from within. Each stretch mark and skin change is a symbol of the life growing inside you, a sign of your body's strength and resilience. These *"stripes"* are badges of honor, marking the incredible journey you are on.

Embrace the idea of *"owning your stripes."* Just as a tiger's stripes are a unique part of its identity, your stretch marks are a unique part of your story. They represent the strength and courage it takes to bring new life into the world. Celebrate them as symbols of your journey and the miracle of your body's ability to nurture and sustain life.

Consider practicing self-care routines to help you feel more comfortable and confident. Moisturize your skin, stay hydrated, and wear comfortable clothing that makes you feel good. Talking with your partner or a close friend about how you're feeling can also provide comfort and reassurance.

Remember, the changes in your body are temporary and are part of the beautiful process of creating new life. Embrace these changes with gratitude and see them as a part of your unique journey.

Mom's Moments

Describe your initial reaction to noticing stretch marks or other skin changes. Reflect on how your perspective can shift towards acceptance and self-love. Embrace and "own your stripes" as symbols of your strength and beauty, using affirmations to reinforce your positive mindset.

Short Prayer

Dear God, help me to embrace the changes in my body with acceptance and self-love. Remind me of the beauty in my journey and the miracle of my baby. Amen.

_____

_____

_____

_____

27

PREPARING FOR MATERNITY LEAVE

"In their hearts humans plan their course, but the Lord establishes their steps."

— PROVERBS 16:9

Are you planning for your maternity leave and feeling the pressure of balancing work and preparation for your baby? The transition into maternity leave can be a time of mixed emotions, filled with excitement and anxiety. It's a period that requires careful planning and trust in God's guidance.

Reflecting on Proverbs 16:9, we are reminded that while we make our plans, it is the Lord who establishes our steps. Start by discussing your plans with your employer, understanding your maternity leave rights, and setting up a clear timeline for your departure. It's helpful to create a detailed plan for your work responsibilities to ensure a smooth handover.

Make a checklist of tasks you need to complete before your leave, both at work and home. This might include setting up the nursery, finalizing your birth plan, and organizing baby essentials. Communicate openly with your partner about your needs and expectations during this time.

While it's important to plan, also leave room for flexibility. Trust that God will guide your steps and provide you with the wisdom and strength you need during this transition.

Mom's Moments

Outline your current plans for maternity leave. Reflect on any concerns or uncertainties you have and write a few sentences seeking guidance and balance in your preparation.

Short Prayer

Dear God, guide me as I prepare for maternity leave. Help me to balance work and preparation for my baby, and establish my steps with Your wisdom. Amen.

28

DEALING WITH PREGNANCY BRAIN

"But he said to me, 'My grace is sufficient for you, for my power is made perfect in weakness.' Therefore I will boast all the more gladly about my weaknesses, so that Christ's power may rest on me."

— 2 CORINTHIANS 12:9

Are you experiencing forgetfulness or "pregnancy brain"? It's a common part of pregnancy, often leaving you feeling frustrated or even embarrassed. This phase can be challenging, but it's also an opportunity to show yourself grace and patience.

Pregnancy brain can make you feel scattered, forgetting appointments, misplacing items, or struggling to recall simple details. It's important to remember that these lapses are temporary and a normal part of your body's incredible work in nurturing new life. Instead of succumbing to frustration, embrace this time as a chance to slow down and prioritize what truly matters.

Consider Mary, who faced overwhelming experiences during her pregnancy. Luke 2:19 tells us that she pondered and treasured these moments in her heart. Mary didn't allow the chaos around her to cause anxiety; instead, she found strength in quiet reflection and acceptance. Similarly, you can find strength in acknowledging and embracing these moments of forgetfulness.

Practical strategies can help manage pregnancy brain. Keep a notepad or digital calendar handy to jot down important reminders. Laugh at the moments of forgetfulness and share these humorous anecdotes with loved ones. Allow yourself to lean on the support of those around you, and remember, it's okay to ask for help.

This is a temporary phase in your journey. By embracing it with grace and humor, you can find joy and strength in the midst of forgetfulness. God's grace is sufficient for you, and His power is made perfect in your weakness.

Mom's Moments

Reflect on your experiences with forgetfulness. Write about how you can show yourself patience and grace during this time. Consider practical strategies to manage pregnancy brain, such as using a planner, setting reminders, and creating checklists. Embrace this phase with humor and acceptance, acknowledging it as a temporary and unique part of your pregnancy journey.

Short Prayer

Dear God, Grant me patience and grace as I navigate forgetfulness during pregnancy. Help me to rely on Your strength and cherish this unique journey. Amen.

_____

_____

POSITIVE AFFIRMATIONS FOR EXPECTANT MOTHERS

Introduction:

Affirmations are powerful tools to cultivate a positive mindset during your pregnancy. Repeat these affirmations daily to build confidence, reduce anxiety, and strengthen your connection with your baby.

Affirmations:

1. I am strong, capable, and ready for motherhood.
2. My body is designed to nourish and protect my baby.
3. Every day, I am becoming a more loving and attentive mother.
4. I trust in the natural process of pregnancy and childbirth.
5. My baby is healthy, happy, and growing beautifully.
6. I am surrounded by love and support.
7. I embrace the changes in my body with gratitude and joy.
8. I listen to my body's needs and take care of myself.
9. I am connected to my baby and feel their presence every day.
10. I am at peace and excited about the journey ahead.

Reflection Space:

How do these affirmations make you feel? Write down your thoughts and any personal affirmations that resonate with you.

_____

_____
_____
_____
_____
_____
_____
_____

GUIDED VISUALIZATIONS FOR CONNECTING WITH YOUR BABY

Introduction:

Visualization exercises can help you connect with your baby and create a sense of calm and peace. These guided visualizations are designed to strengthen your bond and prepare you emotionally for motherhood.

Visualization Exercises:

1. **Meeting Your Baby:**
   Find a quiet place and sit comfortably. Close your eyes and take a few deep breaths. Imagine yourself in a peaceful, beautiful place. Visualize holding your baby in your arms for the first time. Feel their warmth, see their tiny features, and experience the overwhelming love and joy. Take a few moments to savor this connection.

2. **Your Safe Haven:**
   Close your eyes and breathe deeply. Picture a serene, safe place where you feel completely at ease. Imagine yourself and your baby in this haven, surrounded by love and light. Feel the peace and tranquility washing over you. This is your safe space to retreat to whenever you need calm and reassurance.

3. **Bonding with Your Baby:**
   Sit in a comfortable position and close your eyes. Place your hands on your belly and take deep, slow breaths. Visualize a golden thread connecting your heart to your baby's heart. With each breath, feel the bond between you growing stronger. Send your baby love, warmth, and positive energy through this connection.

Reflection Space:

How did the visualizations make you feel? Write down your experiences and any personal insights gained from these exercises.

_____
_____
_____
_____
_____
_____

29

HANDLING UNWANTED COMMENTS ABOUT YOUR BODY

"The tongue has the power of life and death, and those who love it will eat its fruit."

— PROVERBS 18:21

How do you handle unwanted comments about your body during pregnancy? People often feel entitled to share their opinions, which can sometimes be hurtful or unwelcome. Comments like *"Are you sure you're not having twins?"* or *"You look so much bigger than last time!"* can affect your self-esteem and overall sense of well-being.

Proverbs 18:21 reminds us that words have the power of life and death. It's important to protect your heart from negative comments and to respond with grace and confidence. When someone makes an unwelcome comment about your body, take a deep breath and remind yourself of the incredible work your body is doing. You are nurturing and growing a new life, and that is a beautiful, powerful thing.

Responding with kindness can also disarm negativity. A simple, *"I appreciate your concern, but I feel good about my progress,"* can be both respectful and assertive. Surround yourself with positive, supportive people who uplift and encourage you. Practice positive self-talk and remind yourself of the beauty and strength in your changing body.

Remember, your body is doing miraculous work, and each change is a testament to God's incredible design. Embrace these changes with confidence, knowing that you are beautifully and wonderfully made.

Mom's Moments

Write about aspects of your body that you are grateful for and that you love. Reflect on how focusing on gratitude can help you handle negative comments. Pray for a heart filled with gratitude and self-love.

Short Prayer

Dear God, help me to respond to unwanted comments with grace and confidence. Strengthen my self-image and remind me of the beauty in my journey. Amen.

30

ENJOYING THE SECOND TRIMESTER GLOW

"Those who look to him are radiant; their faces are never covered with shame."

— PSALM 34:5

Are you experiencing the famous "second trimester glow"? This phase of pregnancy often brings a sense of well-being and noticeable physical changes that can make you feel beautiful. I remember looking in the mirror and noticing a new radiance in my skin, a glow that seemed to reflect the joy and excitement growing inside me.

Reflecting on Psalm 34:5, we see a beautiful reminder that those who look to God are radiant. This verse isn't just about physical appearance; it's about the inner light that comes from being filled with God's love and joy. The second trimester can be a time when this inner light shines through, manifesting as that pregnancy glow everyone talks about.

Embrace this time and celebrate the positive changes in your body. Enjoy the compliments and let them remind you of the miraculous work happening within you. Use this period to nourish yourself—

both physically and spiritually. Eating well, staying hydrated, and spending time in prayer and reflection can enhance this feeling of radiance.

Take a moment each day to appreciate this special glow. It's a reflection of the incredible journey you're on and the beautiful life growing inside you.

Mom's Moments

Reflect on a day when you felt particularly beautiful or energized. Write down the details of that day, including what you did, what you wore, and how you felt. Consider keeping a journal or photo diary to capture these glowing moments throughout your pregnancy.

Short Prayer

Dear God, thank You for the beautiful glow I feel during this second trimester. I am grateful for the radiance that comes from Your love and the joy of expecting my baby. Amen.

31

CREATING THE PERFECT NURSERY

"By wisdom a house is built, and through understanding it is established; through knowledge its rooms are filled with rare and beautiful treasures."

— PROVERBS 24:3-4

Are you preparing a special place for your baby's arrival? Setting up the nursery is one of the most exciting parts of pregnancy. It's a way to create a nurturing and loving environment for your baby. Reflecting on the story of preparing a place for Jesus' birth can provide inspiration and perspective.

Joseph and Mary prepared for Jesus' birth in the humblest of settings—a manger. Despite the simplicity, it was a place filled with love, warmth, and the presence of God. As you prepare your baby's nursery, remember that it's not about how grand or perfect the space is, but the love and care you put into it.

Proverbs 24:3-4 reminds us that wisdom, understanding, and knowledge fill a home with beautiful treasures. As you plan and decorate, pray for guidance and wisdom. Here are some practical tips to consider:

1. **Safety First:** Choose furniture that meets safety standards. Ensure cribs, changing tables, and other items are sturdy and free from hazards.
2. **Comfort & Functionality:** Arrange the room for easy access to essentials. A comfortable chair for feeding, a well-stocked changing area, and accessible storage can make daily routines smoother.
3. **Calming Atmosphere:** Use soft colors and gentle lighting to create a peaceful environment. Consider adding a white noise machine or soft music to help soothe your baby.
4. **Personal Touches:** Incorporate elements that reflect your family's faith and values. Inspirational art, a small bookshelf with favorite childhood books, or a special corner for prayer can make the room feel spiritually nurturing.
5. **Flexibility:** Plan for the room to grow with your baby. Choose versatile furniture and decor that can adapt as your child grows.

During my pregnancy, I found great joy in setting up the nursery. Each item I placed and each detail I attended to felt like an act of love and preparation for the baby I was eagerly awaiting.

Mom's Moments

Spend some time visualizing your ideal nursery. What colors, themes, and decorations do you imagine? Sketch or write down your vision. Reflect on how you want the space to feel for both you and your baby. Pray for guidance in making this place ready for your baby's arrival.

BIBLICAL TEACHINGS

Short Prayer

Dear God, guide me as I prepare the nursery for my baby. Help me to create a space filled with love, peace, and Your presence. Amen.

32

EXPERIENCING EMOTIONAL STABILITY

> *"But the fruit of the Spirit is love, joy, peace, forbearance, kindness, goodness, faithfulness, gentleness and self-control. Against such things there is no law."*
>
> — GALATIANS 5:22-23

Are you noticing moments of emotional stability and peace during your pregnancy? Pregnancy can be an emotional rollercoaster, but there are times when you feel a profound sense of calm and balance. These moments of stability are a blessing, allowing you to connect more deeply with your baby and experience the joy of your pregnancy.

Reflecting on Galatians 5:22-23, we see that the fruit of the Spirit includes peace and self-control. These gifts are particularly precious during pregnancy, offering you a respite from anxiety and stress. Embrace these moments and recognize them as a sign of God's presence in your life.

To foster emotional stability, consider incorporating some natural strategies into your routine. Spend time in prayer and meditation, asking God to fill you with His peace. Practice deep breathing exercises or prenatal yoga to help manage stress and promote relaxation. Engage in activities that bring you joy and fulfillment, whether it's taking a walk in nature, reading a good book, or spending quality time with loved ones.

Surround yourself with supportive people who uplift and encourage you. Talking about your feelings with a trusted friend, family member, or support group can provide comfort and reassurance. Remember, it's okay to ask for help and to lean on others during this time.

Mom's Moments

Take a few minutes each day to reflect on your emotions. Write down moments when you felt calm, joyful, or at peace. Reflect on what contributed to these feelings and how you can cultivate them more often.

Short Prayer

Dear God, thank You for the moments of emotional stability and peace. Help me to embrace these times and to nurture my well-being. Amen.

_____

_____

_____

_____

_____

_____

BONDING ACTIVITIES AND COMMUNICATION EXERCISES WITH YOUR PARTNER

Joint activities:

Joint Baby Preparations: Spend time together preparing for the baby's arrival. Set up the nursery, shop for baby essentials, or attend prenatal classes together. These activities help you both feel involved and connected.

Daily Check-Ins: Set aside time each day to talk about your feelings, concerns, and excitement. Open communication fosters understanding and support.

Massage and Relaxation: Give each other massages to relieve stress and promote relaxation. Consider taking a prenatal massage class.

Cook Together: Plan and prepare healthy meals together. It promotes healthy eating and gives you quality time to bond.

Exercise as a Team: Engage in light physical activities like walking, yoga, or swimming together. Exercising as a team encourages a healthy lifestyle and gives you quality time to connect.

Date Night Ideas for Pregnant Couples:

Home Spa Night: Create a relaxing spa experience at home with candles, soft music, and massages. Pamper each other and unwind together.

Picnic Indoors: Set up a cozy indoor picnic with all your favorite foods. Enjoy a meal together in a relaxed, intimate setting.

Movie Marathon: Choose a series of movies or TV shows you both enjoy and have a movie marathon night. Make it special with homemade popcorn and comfy blankets.

Memory Lane: Spend an evening looking through old photos and reminiscing about your journey together. Share your favorite memories and discuss your excitement for the future.

Communication Exercises:

Active Listening: Practice active listening by giving your partner your full attention when they speak. Reflect back what you hear to ensure understanding.

Expressing Gratitude: Regularly express appreciation for each other. Share three things you are grateful for about your partner each day.

Future Planning: Discuss your hopes and dreams for your family. Talk about how you envision your lives changing with the baby's arrival.

Conflict Resolution: Learn and practice healthy ways to resolve conflicts. Use "I" statements to express your feelings without blaming and work together to find solutions.

BONDING ACTIVITIES AND DATE NIGHT TRACKER

Date	What We Did	How We Felt

33

HANDLING UNEXPECTED MEDICAL CONCERNS

> *"So do not fear, for I am with you; do not be dismayed, for I am your God. I will strengthen you and help you; I will uphold you with my righteous right hand."*
>
> — ISAIAH 41:10

Have you faced unexpected medical concerns during your pregnancy? These moments can be incredibly stressful and frightening. I remember when I encountered unexpected complications during my pregnancy. The fear and uncertainty were overwhelming, but leaning on God's promises provided strength and comfort.

Isaiah 41:10 offers a powerful reminder that God is with us, even in the most challenging times. When I faced medical concerns, I found solace in knowing that God was by my side, ready to strengthen and uphold me. Each doctor's visit and each test result was an opportunity to trust in His care.

Practical steps can also help manage these concerns. Communicate openly with your healthcare provider, ask questions, and seek a second opinion if needed. Surround yourself with a support system of family and friends who can offer comfort and prayers. Most importantly, continue to pray and seek God's guidance, trusting that He is in control.

During my pregnancy, I learned to balance medical advice with faith. I took the necessary medical steps while constantly praying for God's healing and protection. This dual approach provided a sense of control and peace.

Mom's Moments

Write about any medical concerns that have arisen during your pregnancy. Reflect on how you can trust in God's care and seek His strength. Pray for healing and peace in His presence.

Short Prayer

Dear God, please heal me and protect my baby from any medical concerns. I trust in Your care and strength, knowing You are always with us. Amen.

34

STRESS-FREE BABY REGISTRY

> *"Therefore I tell you, do not worry about your life, what you will eat or drink; or about your body, what you will wear. Is not life more than food, and the body more than clothes? Look at the birds of the air; they do not sow or reap or store away in barns, and yet your heavenly Father feeds them. Are you not much more valuable than they?"*
>
> — MATTHEW 6:25-27

Are you feeling overwhelmed by baby registries and the preparations for your little one? The lists of must-haves and endless options can be daunting, leaving you anxious and stressed about getting everything right. It's easy to get caught up in the details and lose sight of the joy and anticipation of welcoming your baby.

Reflecting on Matthew 6:25-27, Jesus reminds us not to worry about our needs because God will provide. This passage encourages us to focus on what truly matters and trust that God will take care of the rest. When you feel overwhelmed by baby registries, take a step back and remind yourself that your love and care for your baby are what matter most.

To simplify the process, consider these practical steps:

1. **Prioritize Essentials:** Focus on the items that your baby will need immediately, such as a crib, car seat, and basic clothing. Other items can be added later as needed.
2. **Seek Advice:** Talk to experienced moms about what they found most useful. They can provide insights that simplify your choices.
3. **Set Limits:** Choose a few trusted brands or stores to limit your options and reduce decision fatigue.
4. **Trust Yourself:** Remember that you know what's best for your baby. Trust your instincts and don't feel pressured to follow every trend or recommendation.

Mom's Moments

Remember that your registry doesn't have to be perfect. Focus on practicality and what works best for you and your baby. Letting go of perfectionism can ease your stress. Consider asking other parents for what their best advice would be.

Short Prayer

Dear God, help me to find clarity and simplicity in preparing for my baby. Guide me to focus on what truly matters and trust in Your provision. Amen.

_____

_____

_____

35

MOM-TO-MOM

"Then they can urge the younger women to love their husbands and children."

— TITUS 2:4

Have you experienced the invaluable support of other mothers during your pregnancy? I remember how the wisdom and encouragement from experienced moms made a significant difference in my journey. Their insights and shared experiences provided comfort and guidance, making the path ahead seem less daunting.

Reflecting on Titus 2:4, we see the importance of older women guiding and supporting the younger ones. This verse highlights the beauty of community and the wisdom that comes from those who have walked the path before us. The support from other mothers can be a source of strength, helping you navigate the challenges and joys of pregnancy and motherhood.

During my pregnancy, I found solace in the advice and companionship of other moms. They shared practical tips, listened to my concerns, and reassured me that I was not alone. Their stories and experiences were a reminder of the collective wisdom that exists within the community of mothers.

Embrace this support and seek out connections with other moms. Join a local or online support group, attend prenatal classes, or simply reach out to friends who are mothers. Their support can provide invaluable encouragement and wisdom.

Mom's Moments

Write about the support you have received from other mothers. Reflect on how their guidance has helped you and pray for continued support and wisdom from those who have gone before you.

Short Prayer

Dear God, thank You for the support of other mothers. Bless these relationships and continue to provide wisdom and guidance through their experiences. Amen.

_____

_____

_____

_____

_____

_____

_____

_____

36

MAKING THE MOST OF PARENTAL CLASSES

"Let the wise listen and add to their learning, and let the discerning get guidance."

— PROVERBS 1:5

Have you discovered the excitement and joy that come with attending prenatal classes? These sessions are more than just informative—they offer a chance to connect with other expectant parents and to build your confidence as you prepare for your baby's arrival.

Proverbs 1:5 reminds us of the importance of listening and learning. In prenatal classes, you're doing just that—gaining wisdom and guidance for the journey ahead. These classes cover everything from childbirth techniques to newborn care, providing you with practical knowledge and reassurance.

Think about the first time you attended a class. The room filled with other expectant parents, all sharing the same mixture of anticipation and nervousness. As you listened to the instructor, you felt a sense of camaraderie and relief, knowing you weren't alone in this journey. Each session has likely offered new insights and tips that have boosted your confidence and made you feel more prepared.

Prenatal classes are also a wonderful opportunity to bond with your partner. Working together on breathing exercises, discussing birthing plans, and simply sharing the experience can strengthen your relationship and deepen your connection. Additionally, the friendships you form with other parents-to-be can provide a support network that extends beyond the classes.

Embrace the learning process and find joy in the preparation. Remember, every piece of knowledge you gain is a step towards becoming the best parent you can be. The skills and confidence you build now will help you face the challenges of parenthood with grace and assurance.

Mom's Moments

Take notes during your prenatal class on topics that you find particularly interesting or helpful. After the class, review your notes and identify one or two key takeaways.

Short Prayer

Dear God, thank You for the wisdom and knowledge gained from prenatal classes. Help me to apply this learning and feel confident as I prepare for my baby's arrival. Amen.

_____

_____

_____

_____

THIRD TRIMESTER
What To Expect

Physical Changes:

Braxton Hick Contractions (practice contractions preparing your body for labor), potential swelling in feet and ankles, back pain, shortness of breath (baby pressing against your diaphragm), frequent urination.

Emotional Changes:

Nesting instinct (a desire to clean and organize in preparation for your baby's arrival), excitement and anxiety, mood swings.

Baby's Development:

Weeks 29-32: Rapid brain development, baby begins to control body temperature.
Weeks 33-36: Baby's bones are fully developed, but still soft.
Weeks 37-40: Baby drops lower into the pelvis in preparation for birth.

Health & Nutrition Tips

Iron-Rich Foods: Include lean meats, spinach, and fortified cereals to prevent anemia.
Hydration: Continue to drink plenty of water to stay hydrated.
Small, Frequent Meals: Helps with heartburn and keeps energy levels steady.

Important Milestones

Baby Shower: Celebrating with friends and family.
Final Prenatal Appointments: Monitoring your and the baby's health.
Packing the Hospital Bag: Getting ready for the big day.

THIRD TRIMESTER MILESTONES
Document Your Journey

Baby Shower:
Date: _____

Highlights: _____

_____

_____

Final Prenatal Appointment:
Date: _____

Doctor's Notes: _____

_____

_____

Hospital Bag Packing:
Date: _____

Essentials Packed: _____

_____

_____

Nursery Completion:
Date: _____

Reflection: How do you feel as the big day approaches? Write down your thoughts, feelings, and hopes.

_____

_____

_____

_____

_____

_____

37

COUNTING DOWN THE DAYS

"But if we hope for what we do not yet have, we wait for it patiently."

— ROMANS 8:25

Are you eagerly counting down the days until your baby's arrival? The final weeks of pregnancy are filled with dreams and hopes, mixed with a touch of impatience and excitement. This time can be a whirlwind of emotions, from excitement to nervousness. Waiting can be challenging, but it is also a precious time to prepare your heart and home for the new addition.

Romans 8:25 encourages us to embrace patience as we wait for what we hope for. Just as a gardener waits for the seeds to sprout and grow, nurturing them with care, you are nurturing your baby with every passing day. This waiting period is a chance to reflect on your hopes and dreams for your child and to pray for their future.

Think about how Mary, the mother of Jesus, must have felt as she awaited His birth. Her heart was filled with wonder, hope, and a bit of uncertainty. Yet, she trusted in God's plan and embraced the waiting period with faith. You too can use this time to prepare spiritually and emotionally, finding joy in the little moments and trusting in God's perfect timing.

This is also a wonderful opportunity to focus on self-care and bonding with your partner. Engage in activities that bring you joy and relaxation, such as reading a good book, taking gentle walks, or enjoying a quiet evening together. Make time for meaningful conversations about your hopes and dreams for your baby, and pray together for the journey ahead.

Use this waiting period to prepare your home and heart for your baby's arrival. Set up the nursery, organize baby clothes, and gather essentials, but also take time to reflect on the emotional and spiritual aspects of welcoming a new life into your family. Trust that each day brings you closer to the moment you will hold your precious baby in your arms.

Mom's Moments

Take a few moments each day to sit quietly, place your hands on your belly, and talk to your baby. Share your hopes, sing a lullaby, or simply express your love and excitement for their arrival.

Short Prayer

Dear God, Help me to embrace the anticipation of my baby's arrival with patience and joy. Fill my heart with hope and peace as I prepare for this new chapter. Amen.

38

GOD'S STRENGTH FOR LABOR

> *"He gives strength to the weary and increases the power of the weak. Even youths grow tired and weary, and young men stumble and fall; but those who hope in the Lord will renew their strength. They will soar on wings like eagles; they will run and not grow weary, they will walk and not be faint."*
>
> — ISAIAH 40:29-31

Have you ever wondered how you will find the strength to endure labor and delivery? The thought of giving birth can be daunting, filled with both fear and excitement. Reflecting on the strength that God provides can bring immense comfort and reassurance.

Consider the story of Mary, the mother of Jesus. As she approached the time to give birth, far from home and in less than ideal conditions, she relied on God's strength. Her journey was not easy, yet she trusted in God's plan and found the strength to bring the Savior into the world. This profound trust and reliance on God's strength is something we can all learn from.

Isaiah 40:29-31 reminds us that God gives strength to the weary and power to the weak. As you prepare for labor, remember that you do not have to rely on your own strength alone. God is with you, ready to renew your strength and carry you through this challenging time.

During my own labor, I found myself praying constantly, asking God for the strength to endure each contraction and the courage to face the unknown. Each prayer was met with a sense of peace and empowerment, reminding me that I was not alone.

Reflect on times in your life when God has given you strength. Use these memories as a source of encouragement as you approach labor and delivery. Trust that God will be with you, giving you the strength and endurance you need.

Mom's Moments

Create a playlist of your favorite uplifting and calming songs or hymns that you can listen to during labor. Music can be a powerful tool to help you focus, relax, and draw on God's strength during the process.

Short Prayer

Dear God, thank You for the strength You have given me in the past. Please grant me strength and endurance as I prepare for labor and delivery. Amen.

_____

_____

_____

39

CREATING A SPIRITUAL ENVIRONMENT

"But as for me and my household, we will serve the Lord."

— JOSHUA 24:15

Have you thought about how you will create a spiritually nurturing environment for your baby? As you prepare for this new chapter, consider how you can infuse your home with love, faith, and a sense of peace. This intentional effort can have a lasting impact on your child's spiritual growth and well-being.

Joshua 24:15 is a powerful reminder of the commitment to serve the Lord within your household. Creating a spiritual environment starts with making faith a central part of your family's life. This can be through daily prayers, reading Bible stories, playing worship music, and setting an example of living a Christ-centered life.

When I was expecting my first child, my husband and I spent time praying over the nursery, asking God to fill it with His presence. We placed a small Bible on a shelf, and I found a beautiful framed verse to hang on the wall. These small touches served as daily reminders of God's love and promises.

Think about ways you can invite God's presence into your home. It might be through simple acts like praying together as a family, reading scripture during quiet times, or decorating the nursery with faith-inspired artwork. These elements not only create a comforting atmosphere but also lay a strong spiritual foundation for your child.

As you plan for your baby's arrival, pray for wisdom and inspiration to create a nurturing environment that reflects God's love and grace. Trust that He will guide you in making your home a place where faith can flourish.

Mom's Moments

Plan a regular family devotional time with your partner. Choose a time each week to read a Bible passage, pray together, and discuss how you want to create a spiritually nurturing environment for your baby. This shared practice can strengthen your relationship and spiritual foundation.

Short Prayer

Dear God, help me create a home filled with Your love and presence. Grant me wisdom and inspiration as I prepare a spiritually nurturing environment for my baby. Amen.

40

EMOTIONAL PREP FOR THE BIG DAY

"When I am afraid, I put my trust in you."

— PSALM 56:3

As you approach labor, have you taken time to reflect on your emotions and prepare your heart for this significant event? The anticipation of labor can stir a range of feelings, from excitement and joy to fear and anxiety. It's important to address these emotions and seek God's peace and courage.

During my pregnancies, I experienced a mix of emotions as my due dates approached. There were moments of excitement, imagining holding my baby for the first time, and moments of fear, wondering how I would handle the pain and the unknowns of labor. Psalm 56:3 became a source of comfort, reminding me to trust in God when I felt afraid.

To prepare emotionally, I spent time in prayer, asking God to calm my fears and fill me with His peace. I also found it helpful to talk about my feelings with my husband, friends, and my doctor. Sharing my concerns and hearing words of encouragement helped me feel more supported and less alone.

Consider creating a birth plan that includes not just the physical aspects of labor but also your emotional and spiritual needs. Think about the scriptures, prayers, and affirmations that bring you comfort and strength. You might even prepare a playlist of worship songs that can help keep you calm and focused during labor.

Emotional preparation is just as important as physical preparation. Trust that God will be with you every step of the way, providing the courage and peace you need. Embrace the emotions, knowing that they are part of this incredible journey.

Mom's Moments

Write a letter to yourself expressing your hopes, fears, and expectations for labor. Acknowledge any anxieties you have and offer yourself words of encouragement and support.

Short Prayer

Dear God, please grant me peace and courage as I prepare for labor. Help me to trust in Your presence and be emotionally ready for this journey. Amen.

_____

_____

_____

_____

_____

LABOR AND DELIVERY PREPARATION

Birth Plan Template:

Preferences for Labor:

- Pain Management: _____

- Ambiance (music, lighting, etc.): _____

Delivery Preferences:

- Positions: _____

- Who's Present: _____

- Location (hospital, home, birthing center): _____

- Method (traditional, water birth, etc.): _____

Packing a Hospital Bag:

For You:

- Comfortable Clothing: _____

- Toiletries: _____

- Important Documents: _____

For Baby:

- First Outfit: _____

- Blankets and Swaddles: _____

- Diapers and Wipes: _____

EXERCISES AND BREATHING TECHNIQUES FOR LABOR

Breathing Techniques:
- **Deep Breathing:** Inhale deeply through your nose, expanding your abdomen, and exhale slowly through your mouth.
- **Visualization:** Picture a calming scene or focus on a positive image while breathing deeply.

Exercises:
- **Pelvic Tilts:** Helps relieve back pain and strengthen abdominal muscles.
- **Kegel Exercises:** Strengthens pelvic floor muscles, which can help during delivery.
- **Squats:** Strengthens legs and helps open the pelvis.
- **Prenatal Yoga**: Helps you relax and stay positive during labor, and may reduce the duration of labor and increase the odds of a normal vaginal birth.

41

WELCOMING YOUR BABY

"I prayed for this child, and the Lord has granted me what I asked of him. So now I give him to the Lord. For his whole life he will be given over to the Lord."

—1 SAMUEL 1:27-28

Have you felt the overwhelming anticipation and joy as you prepare to welcome your baby? The final weeks of pregnancy are filled with eager expectations, dreams of holding your little one, and imagining the beautiful moments you will share. This journey of anticipation reminds me of the story of Hannah, who fervently prayed for a child and experienced immense joy when she welcomed her son, Samuel.

Hannah's story is a testament to the power of prayer and the fulfillment of God's promises. Her joy in welcoming Samuel was palpable, a moment she had longed for and cherished. Similarly, your anticipation and joy are building as the day to meet your baby approaches. Each kick, each flutter, and each hiccup are reminders of the precious life growing within you.

Take a moment to reflect on this incredible journey. Write a letter to your baby, expressing your joy, love, and dreams for their future. Share your hopes and aspirations, and let your words be a testament to the love that has grown alongside your baby. Just as Hannah dedicated Samuel to the Lord, you can dedicate your thoughts, prayers, and love to your baby, preparing for the moment when you finally hold them in your arms.

Mom's Moments

Create a special "welcome home" plan for your baby. Prepare a cozy space in your home, gather a few favorite baby clothes, and think about any special traditions or rituals you want to start from day one. This preparation can make the arrival even more meaningful.

Short Prayer

Dear God, thank You for the joy and anticipation I feel as I prepare to meet my baby. Help me to cherish these final weeks and to express my love and joy to my child. Amen.

42

FINDING PEACE AMIDST PRE-BIRTH CHAOS

"Peace I leave with you; my peace I give you. I do not give to you as the world gives. Do not let your hearts be troubled and do not be afraid."

— JOHN 14:27

Are you finding it challenging to maintain peace amidst the chaos of preparing for your baby's arrival? The final weeks can often feel overwhelming, with a flurry of preparations, last-minute tasks, and the weight of anticipation. It's easy to feel swept up in the chaos, but finding moments of peace is crucial for your well-being.

John 14:27 offers a comforting reminder of the peace that Jesus provides. Unlike the temporary peace the world offers, His peace is enduring and reassuring. It calms our hearts and dispels our fears. As you navigate these final weeks, remember to pause and seek this divine peace.

Think about practical ways to create moments of calm amidst the busyness. Simple practices such as taking deep breaths, spending a few quiet moments in prayer, or listening to soothing music can help center your mind and heart. Reflect on the times when you have felt God's peace wash over you and let those memories guide you through any current anxieties.

As you prepare for your baby's arrival, take time to rest and recharge. Allow yourself to step away from the to-do lists and find comfort in the peace that God offers. Remember, amidst the chaos, there is a divine calm waiting for you. Embrace it, and let it carry you through these final weeks.

Mom's Moments

Engage in a mindfulness or meditation practice designed for expectant mothers. Use guided meditations or apps that focus on pregnancy and relaxation. This practice can help you maintain a sense of calm and well-being, even during the most chaotic times.

Short Prayer

Dear God, amidst the chaos, grant me Your peace. Help me to find moments of calm and to rest in Your presence as I prepare for my baby's arrival. Amen.

_____

_____

_____

_____

_____

_____

43

PREGNANCY INSOMNIA

"In peace I will lie down and sleep, for you alone, Lord, make me dwell in safety."

— PSALM 4:8

Are you struggling with sleepless nights as your due date approaches? It's a common experience in the third trimester, when comfort can be hard to find and anxiety about the coming changes can keep you awake. I remember those restless nights all too well, lying awake with thoughts racing through my mind about the baby's arrival, last-minute preparations, and the changes ahead.

One particularly sleepless night, I found myself getting frustrated with my inability to fall asleep. I decided to get up, make myself a cup of herbal tea, and spend some quiet time reflecting on the day. As I sipped my tea, I thought about how important it was to rest, not just for me, but for my baby too. It reminded me that rest doesn't always have to come in the form of sleep; it can also be found in moments of quiet and peace.

Creating a bedtime routine that promotes relaxation can be incredibly helpful. Try incorporating activities such as reading a book, taking a warm bath, or practicing gentle stretches. Also, making your sleep environment as comfortable as possible—whether that means using extra pillows to support your body, keeping the room cool, or using a white noise machine—can make a big difference.

When you find yourself unable to sleep, use that time to focus on the positive aspects of your pregnancy. Reflect on the joy of feeling your baby move, the excitement of meeting them soon, and the support you have around you. Remember, it's okay to take naps during the day if you're not getting enough sleep at night. Your body is doing a tremendous amount of work, and it's important to be gentle with yourself.

Mom's Moments

Limit screen time before bed. The blue light emitted from phones, tablets, and computers can interfere with your ability to fall asleep. Instead, spend the last hour before bed doing a relaxing activity that doesn't involve screens, like journaling or listening to calming music.

Short Prayer

Dear God, help me find restful sleep and peace in these sleepless nights. Guide me to trust in the moments of quiet and rest. Amen.

_____

_____

_____

_____

44

LAST-MINUTE BABY PREP

"Do not be anxious about anything, but in every situation, by prayer and petition, with thanksgiving, present your requests to God. And the peace of God, which transcends all understanding, will guard your hearts and your minds in Christ Jesus."

— PHILIPPIANS 4:6-7

Are you feeling overwhelmed by the stress of last-minute preparations? The third trimester often brings a flurry of activity as you try to get everything ready for your baby's arrival. From setting up the nursery to packing your hospital bag, the to-do list can seem endless.

It's easy to feel stressed when it seems like there's so much left to do. During my pregnancies, I found myself making endless lists, trying to check off each item while still managing daily life. I learned that it was crucial to take a step back and prioritize what truly needed to be done, and to let go of what could wait or wasn't essential.

One strategy that helped was breaking tasks into smaller, more manageable steps. Instead of trying to tackle everything at once, I focused on completing a few key tasks each day. This not only made the list feel less daunting but also gave me a sense of accomplishment as I steadily worked through my preparations.

Remember, it's important to ask for help when you need it. Your partner, family, and friends are likely eager to support you. Delegating tasks can alleviate some of the pressure and allow you to focus on what only you can do.

Take a deep breath and remind yourself that it's okay if everything isn't perfect. Your baby needs your love and care more than a perfectly set-up nursery or meticulously packed hospital bag. Trust that you will have everything you need when the time comes and that it's okay to leave some tasks unfinished if it means preserving your peace and well-being.

Mom's Moments

Create a last-minute preparation checklist. List out all the tasks you need to complete before your baby arrives, prioritizing them by importance. This can help you manage your time more effectively and reduce stress as you see tasks being checked off. Set aside 15 minutes each day to tackle a small task on the list.

Short Prayer

Dear God, help me to manage last-minute preparations with calm and trust. Grant me peace and the ability to prioritize what truly matters. Amen.

POSTPARTUM PLANNING

Postpartum Care and Recovery:

Physical Care:

- **Rest**: Make time to rest and recover.
- **Hydration**: Drink plenty of water to stay hydrated.
- **Nutrition**: Eat a balanced diet to support healing and energy levels.

Emotional Care:

- **Support System**: Reach out to family and friends for support.
- **Self-Care**: Take time for yourself to relax and recharge.
- **Mental Health**: Be aware of postpartum depression and seek help if needed.

Postpartum Essentials:

Nursing Pads ☐	Postpartum Pads ☐
Comfortable Clothing: ☐	Baby Care Items: ☐
_____	_____
_____	_____
_____	_____

Picture of your baby!

PARENTING TIPS AND EARLY BONDING

Parenting Tips:

Feeding:
- **Breastfeeding or formula feeding**: Follow your baby's hunger cues and establish a feeding routine.

Sleeping:
- Create a safe sleep environment and establish a bedtime routine.

Bonding:
- **Skin-to-skin contact**: Helps regulate the baby's temperature and promotes bonding.
- **Talking and Singing**: Helps your baby recognize your voice and stimulates their senses.

Newborn Bonding Activities:

- **Reading to Your Baby**: Choose simple, colorful books.
- **Gentle Massages**: Helps relax your baby and strengthens your bond.
- **Babywearing**: Keeps your baby close and allows you to be hands-free.

Early Experiences:

- First Feeding Experience: _____
  _____
  _____
  _____
  _____

- First Night at Home: _____
  _____
  _____
  _____
  _____

- Special Moments: _____
  _____
  _____
  _____
  _____

45

THIRD TRIMESTER DISCOMFORTS

"But he said to me, 'My grace is sufficient for you, for my power is made perfect in weakness.' Therefore I will boast all the more gladly about my weaknesses, so that Christ's power may rest on me."

— 2 CORINTHIANS 12:9

How are you managing the physical discomforts of the third trimester? As your due date approaches, your body might feel more strained and uncomfortable. This period can be physically challenging, much like Mary's journey to Bethlehem. Imagine Mary, heavily pregnant, traveling a long distance. The discomfort and fatigue she experienced must have been immense, yet she pressed on, trusting in God's plan.

Mary's story reminds us that discomfort and hardship are often part of the journey, but they are also moments where we can find God's strength. In your own pregnancy, these physical challenges can be overwhelming, but remember that God's grace is sufficient for you. Each ache and pain is a reminder of the incredible work your body is doing to bring new life into the world.

To manage physical discomfort, consider incorporating gentle stretches or prenatal yoga into your routine. These can help alleviate tension and improve flexibility. Using supportive pillows while sleeping, taking warm baths, and practicing deep breathing can also provide relief. Listening to your body and taking breaks when needed is essential. Remember, it's okay to slow down and ask for help.

Embrace these moments of discomfort as part of your unique journey. Trust that God's strength is with you, sustaining you through each challenge. Just as Mary found the strength to complete her journey, you too will find the strength to embrace these final weeks with grace and perseverance.

Mom's Moments

Reflect on, and write down, the physical discomforts of the third trimester. Pray for strength and acceptance of your body's changes.

Short Prayer

Dear God, help me to embrace the physical discomforts of this final stage of pregnancy. Grant me strength and patience as my body changes and prepares for birth. Amen.

_____

_____

_____

_____

_____

_____

46

CHERISHING THE LAST DAYS

"Children are a heritage from the Lord, offspring a reward from him."

— PSALM 127:3

Have you taken a moment to savor the final weeks of your pregnancy? This unique time is filled with anticipation and emotion, a period that you will look back on with fondness. I remember the last days of my pregnancies, feeling a mix of excitement, impatience, and nostalgia.

One evening, as I felt my baby moving inside me, I realized how precious these final moments were. I knew that soon I would no longer feel those little kicks and rolls. I decided to cherish each moment, to truly enjoy the experience of carrying my baby. I took walks in the park, talking to my baby, and spent quiet evenings reading and reflecting on the journey we had shared so far.

These last moments of pregnancy are an opportunity to connect deeply with your baby. Take time to rest, to feel each movement, and to reflect on the incredible process of bringing a new life into the world. Write down your thoughts and feelings, capture the beauty of this time in a journal or through photographs.

Allow yourself to slow down and savor these final days. Share your hopes and dreams with your baby, and take comfort in knowing that you are about to embark on an amazing new chapter. These moments are fleeting, but the memories will stay with you forever.

Mom's Moments

Create a memory board. Gather photos, ultrasound images, and mementos from your pregnancy journey. Spend time arranging them on a board or in a scrapbook, reflecting on the special moments and milestones you've experienced. This can help you savor these last weeks and create a keepsake for the future.

Short Prayer

Dear God, thank You for these precious final moments of pregnancy. Help me to savor this time and cherish the connection I have with my baby. Amen.

_____

_____

_____

_____

_____

_____

47

FACING FEARS OF THE UNKNOWN

"So do not fear, for I am with you; do not be dismayed, for I am your God. I will strengthen you and help you; I will uphold you with my righteous right hand."

— ISAIAH 41:10

Are you feeling anxious about the unknown aspects of labor, delivery, and motherhood? It's natural to have fears about what lies ahead, especially when facing something as life-changing as bringing a new baby into the world. I remember how, during my first pregnancy, the anticipation was often overshadowed by fear of the unknown. *What would labor be like? Would my baby be healthy? How would I handle the demands of motherhood?*

One evening, feeling particularly overwhelmed, I opened my Bible to Isaiah 41:10. The verse reminded me that I wasn't alone; God was with me every step of the way. This realization brought a profound sense of peace. I started to focus on the truth that, regardless of the uncertainties, God's presence and strength were constants I could rely on.

Practical steps also helped me manage my fears. I took childbirth classes, talked openly with my healthcare provider about my concerns, and read positive birth stories to help prepare mentally. I also joined a support group for expectant mothers, where sharing fears and hearing others' experiences made me feel less isolated.

When fear starts to creep in, remind yourself that God is with you, ready to strengthen and uphold you. Embrace the journey with faith, knowing that His plan for you and your baby is perfect, even when the details are unclear. Take it one step at a time, leaning on His promises and finding courage in His unwavering support.

Mom's Moments

Practice guided visualization. Spend a few minutes each day visualizing a positive birth experience and peaceful early days with your baby. Imagine yourself handling challenges with grace and ease. This can help reduce anxiety and build confidence.

Short Prayer

Dear God, help me to face my fears of the unknown with courage and trust in Your plan. Strengthen me and uphold me through every step of this journey. Amen.

48

FAITH OVER FINANCES

"And my God will meet all your needs according to the riches of his glory in Christ Jesus."

— PHILIPPIANS 4:19

Are you feeling the weight of financial worries as you prepare for your baby's arrival? It's natural to be concerned about providing for your growing family, especially with the many expenses that come with a new baby. These worries can sometimes overshadow the joy of anticipation, but remember that God is your provider and He is faithful to meet all your needs.

Think about the times in your life when God has provided for you, even in ways you didn't expect. Reflecting on His past faithfulness can help you trust Him with your current concerns. Just as He provided manna for the Israelites in the wilderness, He will provide for you and your baby.

Managing financial worries involves practical steps as well. Create a budget to help you track expenses and identify areas where you can save. Look for community resources or support groups that offer assistance to expectant mothers. Planning ahead can alleviate some of the stress, but remember to bring your concerns to God in prayer, trusting Him to guide and provide.

When financial worries start to feel overwhelming, take a moment to breathe and pray. Ask God for wisdom in managing your finances and for peace in your heart. Trust that He sees your needs and is already working to meet them. Lean on His promises and let His peace guard your heart and mind.

Mom's Moments

Develop a simple financial plan. Outline your expected expenses and income for the next few months. Include categories for baby-related costs, and look for areas where you can save or cut back. Having a plan can help reduce anxiety and increase your sense of control.

Short Prayer

Dear God, help me to trust in Your provision for my financial worries. Grant me wisdom and peace as I prepare for my baby's arrival. Amen.

_____

_____

_____

_____

_____

_____

PASS ON THE BLESSINGS

> *"Therefore encourage one another and build each other up, just as in fact you are doing."*
>
> — 1 THESSALONIANS 5:11

Now that you've completed this book you have a wealth of knowledge, strength, and inspiration to help you navigate the beautiful journey of pregnancy. It's time to share your insights and show other expectant mothers where they can find the same support and encouragement.

Simply by leaving your honest opinion of this book on Amazon, you'll show other expectant mothers where they can find the comfort and guidance they're looking for, helping them to experience peace and joy during this special time.

Thank you for your help. The journey of motherhood is enriched when we share our wisdom and experiences with others – and you're helping us to do just that.

Scan below to leave your review on Amazon.

[Insert QR Code]

Your review is a testament to your journey and a beacon of hope for other women entering or navigating pregnancy.

Thank you for being a part of this community of expectant mothers embracing pregnancy with grace and confidence. May God continue to bless you and your growing family, using you as a light in the lives of others.

With gratitude,

Biblical Teachings

AND SO, THE JOURNEY CONTINUES...

Congratulations on making it through this incredible journey of pregnancy, with all its ups and downs. You've shown remarkable strength and resilience. Whether you're holding your baby in your arms or still eagerly awaiting their arrival, may your heart be filled with joy and anticipation for what's to come.

This journey doesn't end with the birth of your baby; it's just beginning. Continue to seek God's presence in every moment of motherhood. Let the lessons you've learned shape your parenting, nurturing your child with love and faith. Keep growing, loving, and connecting with your child, your family, and your community.

As you move forward, carry with you the peace that comes from knowing God is with you every step of the way. Share your story and the joy you've found with others, becoming a source of encouragement and hope.

Thank you for allowing this devotional to accompany you on this sacred journey. It has been a privilege to walk alongside you. I pray these reflections and prayers will continue to support and inspire

AND SO, THE JOURNEY CONTINUES...

you, drawing you ever closer to God's heart. Always remember that you and your child are deeply loved and cherished.

Embrace the future with confidence, knowing that God's plans for you and your baby are filled with hope and promise. This beautiful chapter of your life is just beginning, and your most fulfilling days are ahead.

With love and prayers,

The team at Biblical Teachings

Made in the USA
Columbia, SC
28 December 2024